SPEC

To my children for allowing me the freedom to be open and honest in hopes that someone will be blessed and their lives changed.

The Smith Family (Lou, Henry, and Leslie)

My sincere thanks and appreciation to Lou, thanks for believing in me, encouraging, coaching and cheering me on to keep moving with this project. You never doubted what the Lord was doing even when I grew weary you held my arms up like Aaron and Hur did Moses. Your passion for ministry and your writing skills have made a dream come true. Your commitment and support were demonstrated by your giving so much of your time and energy until completion. I can never repay you for the many hours you spent and your unselfish ways have proven to be a great friend, and confidante. You caught hold of the Vision, took eleven years of my notes, rearranged and put them together made my dream come true. You did not allow me to abort or have a stillborn in the birth canal. You encouraged me to give birth to this baby that had sat in the birth canal far too long. You would not let me abandon my dream. You were a coach, teach, pastor, and friend. You are an anointed to gift to the body of Christ and your passion for writing gave you hope.

Thanks Henry and Leslie for sharing you wife/mother with me during these last months. I know it was a great sacrifice.

NEW GENERATION CHRISTIAN FELLOWSHIP CHURCH
family and friends.

Thanks to all of you for your never ending prayers, love and support. Without you this book would never have been written. Thanks to each of you for the vote of confidence in my leadership ability. You trusted the God in me enough to connect to this body and truly we have seen miracles with signs and wonders following. All glory goes to God. You made my dream come true. Go ahead and DREAM, it's never too late.

Marlon

Thanks Marlon Villadiego for the great cover design.
You worked faithfully with me until we got to where we needed to be, I know it wasn't easy but we made it through.

THANKS TO ALL OF YOU CHEERLEADERS
FOR ENCOURAGING ME WHILE ON THE JOURNEY
TO MY DESTINY!

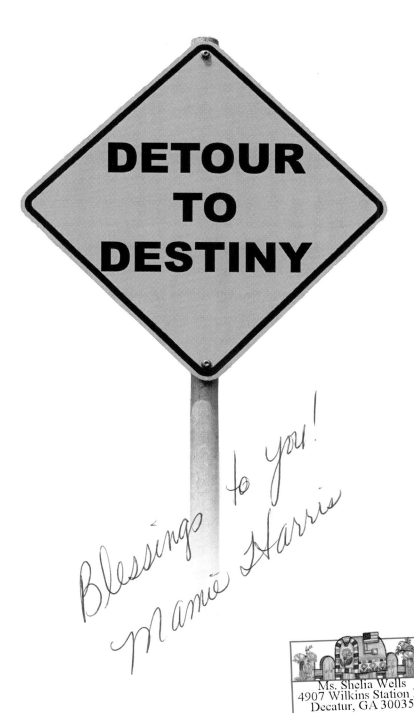

DETOUR
TO
DESTINY

Blessings to you!

Mamie Harris

Ms. Shelia Wells
4907 Wilkins Station Dr
Decatur, GA 30035

Printed in the United States of America

Published by:
Mall Publishing
641 Homewood Avenue
Highland Park, Illinois 60035
1.877.203.2453

Cover Design and Text Design by Marlon B. Villadiego

ISBN 1-934165-19-0

Unless otherwise noted, all scripture quotations are from the New International Version (NIV) of the Holy Bible.

For licensing / copyright information, for additional copies or for use in specialized settings contact:

Mamie Harris
PO Box 1837
Fayetteville, GA 30214
770-716-6025
email: mamieharris@aol.com
www.newgenerationgriffin.org

DETOUR TO DESTINY

MAMIE HARRIS

HIGHLAND PARK, ILLINOIS

TABLE OF CONTENTS

DEDICATION

This book is dedicated to my Lord and Savior Jesus Christ, my deceased husband, Reverend Joseph Harris, and to all hurting people who need healing and restoration.

ACKNOWLEDGEMENT

For several years, I have wanted to write this book as a way to finalize my own grief and to help hurting people. There have been many people in my life who have loved me, inspired me, and supported me through the detours that led to my own destiny. As difficult as life seems at times, God is always with me, orchestrating my path and using people to guide me through my darkest days. I would like to acknowledge the following people.

My husband Joseph Harris was my best friend, the father of my children, my pastor and my mentor. His love and commitment to God, his ministry and our relationship and family, helped me to develop into the person I am today. It is because of his life and sudden death that I was inspired to write this book.

Alma Lowry was my best friend and confidante. She was always there listening to and praying for me. Whenever I came to a crossroad and didn't know who to turn to or what to do, she would always say, "Mamie, just pray and ask God to lead and guide you in the right way." Even though Alma has gone to be with the Lord, she is still an inspiration to me. She was my unpaid counselor and my prayer partner. She taught me family values and social etiquette. I will never forget her trustworthiness and faithfulness and how she and her husband Walter, walked with me through the valleys of my life, and strengthened me when I couldn't stand alone.

Marian Corbin, my friend, coworker and the *Martha* in my life, is always quick to respond and willing to do whatever is needed. Her continual love and support have lasted many years and through many hardships and life challenges. She is like a sister. Because of her loyalty, she has a special place in my heart. She has always included my family in her family gatherings. As a result, we have all become one big extended family. She is a true friend and the epitome of a Christian in action.

Ingrid Delaney, my niece, seems to understand life far beyond what her years would indicate. She is always so positive and understanding and her love and respect for her Uncle Joe and Aunt Mamie gave me the courage to keep my eyes on the Lord.

My nephew Brian Delaney was sent by God to live with us for 13 months until we could deal with the loss of Joe's death. Just his presence in the house gave us a sense of security. I will always cherish his support for my son, Ken, who was a teenager at the time of his father's death. Just having Brian there for the family was invaluable.

Alma Gibbs, my first cousin, is a friend, encourager, and surrogate mother. She has served as a role model for me and her children's accomplishments have spurred me on to achieve in my own life. She was faithful in helping me get through the tough days of my youth and early teens. Alma endorsed my relationship with Joseph and thought we were a great match. Our relationship has remained intact through the years and she will forever hold a special place in my heart.

I thank Linda and Carnell Carr for the joint investment that we made that brought a great return and allowed me to jump-start my life after Joe's death. I am grateful that they did not abandon the family and me when we needed them most. Their confidentiality, spiritual support and compassion will never be forgotten.

Bertha Davis, "Bert", has always reminded me of what I need to do. Through prophetic words, she has warned me of impending dangers and has advised me in practical matters that have kept my family intact financially and emotionally. Her wisdom has helped me tremendously.

Audrey Hughes was a mighty woman of God with a prophetic voice, full of wisdom and knowledge. Early each morning, Audrey would call, have prayer with me and speak truth into my life. She guided me through my grief. Even when I wanted to stay in a state of depression, she challenged me to move forward. In addition to her calls, twice a year she would drive four hours to spend time with me. Her children fondly called me Aunt Mamie. Audrey was a spiritual giant, and was the General in my life – commanding action. We walked through a valley together, hand in hand. She has now gone home to be with the Lord and I miss her greatly.

Sister Roberta Nance, a former pastor's wife who called me almost every month for the last several years and asked, "How are you coming on your book?" She never gave up on my writing the book. Even though I became discouraged along the way, she always inspired me to keep the dream alive. I am eternally grateful to God that she did not give up on the book or me, but walked with me while I was in the valley.

Berdie McCune is my sister, friend and faithful supporter. Berdie and I have always had very different personalities, but she has remained faithful to me. I appreciate how she tried hard to protect me from pain and hurt when we were young children growing up. She looked up to me as her big sister. Since Momma has gone to be with the Lord, she sometimes refers to me as her mother. Berdie has always had confidence in me. She trusts me as her pastor and friend. Even with all the family crises and issues we've faced, we love each other and wish each other the best in life.

Last, but not least, I dedicate this book to my children, Greg, Sonya, Tina and Ken, who have lived their lives as pastor's children and have withstood the sacrifices, scrutiny and sometimes heartaches that come with growing up under the judgment of others. They have survived well, and are happy, successful adults. To God be the glory!

FOREWORD

You hold in your hand an amazing book. It is written with profound transparency by a pastor's widow who by God's grace has persevered and prevailed through unusual hardship. I can think of all kinds of folk who will find this book a unique treasure. It contains romance, crisis, and triumph. Certainly, it will be a welcome and useful guide for recent widows and widowers. It is full of encouragement and insights for those who have lost a life partner. However, all church leaders will find the story of Mamie Harris a thought-provoking account of what can go wrong for the pastor's family and for the church after the sudden loss of the pastor. In addition, just about everyone will find inspiration in this story of Pastor Harris' triumphant struggle.

Pastor Mamie Harris is no ordinary woman. She rose from poverty as a sharecropper's stepdaughter to become a world traveler and a much sought-after conference speaker. The widow of a great pastor, Rev. Joseph Harris, Mamie is herself an excellent teacher and gifted minister of the Gospel. She is a church planting pastor, evangelist and missionary who is recognized for her apostolic vision and spiritual authority. Yet she remains surprisingly unassuming and lives a sacrificially simple lifestyle.

One of the rare honors I have enjoyed in my fifty plus years of ministry is the friendship of this extraordinary lady. My wife Jackie and I became acquainted with Mamie shortly after the loss of her husband Joseph, first as a student, then as an administrative assistant, and later as a fellow missionary.

We have cried, laughed and prayed with her over the years. We were present at the dedication of her new house. She sat with my wife in the hospital when I had surgery. Mamie is one of the individuals in the small inner circle of lifelong friends who we know will always be there for us.

Rejected and isolated by the very church people into whom she and her husband had poured the best years of their lives, Mamie went suddenly from being the First Lady of her church to being an outcast. Devastated by her grief and financial hardship, she found herself unwanted by her own church. Yet her faith never wavered and in her loneliness, she was drawn to an even stronger appreciation of the love of God. She found it to be true that God is the champion of orphans and widows. This faith gave her the courage to leave her government job and step out on faith to plant a church without any promise of an income.

Moreover, she enrolled in Beulah Heights Bible College (Now Beulah Heights University) and began formal training. I first met her as one of my students. As an instructor, I saw her excel as a student in such courses as Old Testament, Hermeneutics and New Testament Epistles. Through divine providence, she became a work-study student and was assigned to work as my administrative assistant. She then became my co-worker in an innovative missionary training program called MOST (Missions Overseas Short Term). She became a MOST team member and traveled with us to conduct MOST training in Kenya, Brazil and South Africa. She has graduated from Beulah Heights, but remains to this day an elder in the student-alumni ministerial association.

In all that time, Mamie has remained consistently a devout Christian woman with inner strength and a calm exterior. No matter what happened, she would wait on God and He would provide. When others were unkind, she remained loving. She let God fight her battles. Others saw her as a strong spiritual leader, and eventually she planted a church and began overseeing other ministries. Today, she is well known and respected in ministry circles. She remains quiet, humble, and loving, but, when she speaks, people listen.

In this book, you will learn the secret to her success. You will read about the price she paid to gain such spiritual maturity. Jesus taught that we must die to self in order to truly live. As you follow her story, you will see how she went through a death to her old life as a First Lady, and slowly, painfully, was delivered into a new life as a spiritual pioneer and a trailblazer for women in ministry.

Above all, this is a book about the loving faithfulness of God, and His unfailing grace that sustains us. It is about letting go and letting God help you get on with the rest of your life. I predict that when you finish reading it, you will want to let go of some things in your life. Then, I think you will want to pass it along to someone else that you know needs to read it too.

Doug Chatham, Ph.D., D. Min.
Director of Graduate Studies,
Beulah Heights University

INTRODUCTION

Detour to Destiny

A friend of mine once told me a story from her childhood about how she and her siblings played in their back yard under a large oak tree. They would explore every inch of the enormous exposed roots and the surrounding area underneath the tree. They found great pleasure in playing a game their mother had taught them: finding the doodlebugs. They would look for a small round indention in the sand that was in the shape of a "V." They would take a small stick or broom straw and gently stir in the circle while chanting, "Doodlebug, Doodlebug, come out. Your house is on fire! Doodlebug, Doodlebug, come out. Your house is on fire!" Eventually, to their amazement, a small, round bug, all scrunched up and looking scared, would surface. The small bug had no idea what they were saying, or what was happening, but because his place of security had been disturbed, he had been exposed and he could no longer hide under the sand. He had to move forward and find his way.

This childhood story reminds me of my own life. I found a place of security beneath the covering of my husband and pastor, only to be stirred out of my comfort zone by his death. Despite my rejection, financial struggles, and loneliness, I had to make sense of my life and move forward. This book is the story of my coming into my own as a person and pastor, after learning through tribulations and tests that no earthly person knows us as well as God does, and that we cannot "hitch our wagon" to anyone except Him. He is the only one who knows assuredly why we were born and why we are passing through this earth.

My story began when I was born out of wedlock to a young mother who was herself the product of an unwanted pregnancy. It seemed that our lives were the result of a chain of sexual mishaps that produced rejection, pain, and hostility in the hearts of the women in my family. It seemed that this, too, would be my destiny.

As the oldest of three children, and the only one born out of wedlock, I was required to take on adult responsibilities at an early age. I never quite fit anywhere because I was caught between the worlds of childhood and adulthood. I never really experienced the joys of being a child. I remember living mostly under judgment, tirelessly trying to please my mother.

My mother loved me in her own way, but in a way that was difficult for a child to recognize. She was a hard, determined woman who could achieve almost anything, but she often left a trail of casualties. She didn't know how to show affection or how to nurture the sensitive needs of a child who had unmet needs, unresolved issues, and unhealed hurts. My quest to find love led me to the arms of a man who sexually exploited and sought to control me, and then left me pregnant and alone. I grew to dislike myself and developed feelings of humiliation, degradation, anger, and a desire for revenge.

Before marrying, I had made a vow to God that if He would send me a husband to take care of my unborn child and me, and if He would help me be a good wife and mother, I would devote my life to doing just that. Two years later, I married my husband, Joe, whom I met when I was seven months pregnant. I found a place of refuge and comfort for 34 years as his wife, and the mother of his children. For 17 years, I was the pastor's wife, and finally, became his widow. During the years of our marriage, I spent most of my time and energy trying to live up to the promise I had made to God.

Just as a mother hen hovers over her chicks and hides them under her wings, I protected my family and children, always watching for any impending harm. Still scarred from my past, and struggling internally, I had trouble trusting anyone, even Joe who had shown me such kindness. Consumed by past hurts, rejection, and low self-esteem, I didn't think I deserved him. I thought he must have had a hidden motive. Clearly, I had emotional problems; nevertheless, I put much effort into trying to live a normal life.

Gradually, God brought me out of this dark path. His unconditional love shone upon my heart, reflecting His goodness and faithfulness. He showed me His example of forgiveness and extended His arm of peace and comfort. Since being liberated from bondage, I have found that every day that I live is an opportunity to become a better version of myself and to love and encourage others to do the same. My purpose in writing this book is to:

- testify of my own healing from a past of emotional and physical pain,
- encourage and inspire others to embrace hardships and challenges as opportunities for success,
- help widows, widowers and others who have lost loved ones, to recover and move on with life,

- inspire those trapped in generational curses (negative life patterns repeated from one generation to another) to gather the strength to break the chains of bondage,
- help hurting people to learn forgiveness, and to pursue and find peace,
- exhort, encourage, and comfort pastors, leaders, their spouses and their children,
- and challenge readers to search the hidden paths of their lives and to follow the detours that may lead to their own destiny.

In chapter 8, you will find my message to hurting people. In addition, the appendix includes a list of tips to help family members plan in advance for the loss of a loved one. The experience of losing my husband has given me the desire to help others who may experience a similar situation.

I have put many disappointments and much anger behind me in an effort to walk in peace and love. I encourage you to do the same and to truly experience the joy of life that comes with releasing people and hurtful past experiences. I am grateful now for every challenge that I had to go through. As a pastor, I can empathize with others and understand that they, too, are on the battlefield of life. Throughout this book, you will see my life's journey unfold as you travel with me through the winding roads and detours that led to my destiny.

THE SHOCK

Thursday started as it always had. I woke up at 4:30 in the morning, spent time with the Lord in prayer, and prepared for work. I stood in my closet for what seemed like hours, trying to pick out what I was going to wear. It was December 12, 1996, a little warm for that time of year. However, it wasn't the weather or my wardrobe that delayed me. My husband, Joe, had been playfully distracting me all morning. He had been very playful lately, tickling me, nudging me, making me laugh as I washed up and brushed my hair. This time he caught me at the closet, staring blankly at a row of blouses.

"I think I'll work in the yard today." he said. "It might rain this weekend and I want to get the cars cleaned up."

I nodded absently as I picked out a purple wool suit and a green blouse. Joe stood there for a moment until I turned to look at him.

"Show me how to start the washer so I can wash the towels for the cars."

A smile spread across my face as I brushed past him. He quickly followed as we went to the washroom. I had shown him how to do laundry many times with the machine. With the patience of a mom showing her children how to do laundry for the first time, I said, "Put the towels in the washer, pour the detergent here, turn this knob and press here. That's all there is to it." I motioned to leave. I was really running late now.

"Wait," he said as he stared at the pile of towels on the machine. "Do you put bleach in these?"

"No. Do you want me to start them for you?

"No I can do it."

With a slight grin, I said, "I've got to go. I'll talk to you later."

I gave him a quick kiss and rushed to get dressed.

I left for work and arrived safely. Normally, I would call home and wake Joe up, but since he was already awake, I didn't bother. I knew that he would be working outside and would eventually call me. We always talked several times throughout the day. I never really told him, but I really looked forward to hearing his voice. The weather forecast was cloudy, so I didn't bother to call earlier in the day. By 1:30 that afternoon, I still hadn't heard from him, which was very unusual. I thought maybe he had finished his work in the yard and decided to visit his mother in Griffin, Georgia. He visited her every day, sometimes twice a day.

There was still no word by 1:45 P.M. I left the office early, called home and left a message reminding him of my appointment at the beauty shop. I left the number and asked him to call me there. All the while I was talking into the machine I wondered, *Where is Joe? Why hasn't he called?* For a second I thought of calling his sister, Ruth, to see if he was there, but decided against it. *I'll wait until I get to the shop,* I said to myself. *Maybe he'll call by then.* After all, I didn't need to worry anyone unnecessarily. Thirty minutes later, I arrived at the beauty shop. Before I sat in the chair, I anxiously asked my beautician, Classie, if Joe had called. She looked at me quizzically.

"No. Is everything ok?"

"I don't know," I responded.

Suddenly, I heard myself repeating everything I had said to myself. "I haven't heard from him all day. He's supposed to be working in the yard today. I've left messages at home for him to call. Maybe he's at his sister's house visiting his mom." I let out a sigh. "I thought he would have called me back by now."

Trying to help dispel my concern, Classie said, "Joe probably left the house early to visit his mom and forgot to call. Maybe he even went shopping for your Christmas presents. Let's get you finished up and out of here. He'll call you before you know it." She held this hopeful smile as I looked at her reflection in the mirror. I felt silly for worrying so much, but I just couldn't shake the feeling that something was wrong.

The whole time I was there my mind stayed on Joe. I called home at least three times to see if he had retrieved my messages. He hadn't. As the hours passed, it became even more unusual. Around 4:20 P.M, Classie was adding some final touches to my hair. I still felt silly for worrying so much. I thought it might help if I did a little Christmas shopping on Memorial Drive. Joe had reminded me a few days earlier to go ahead and get my shopping out of the way.

"Classie," I said. "I'm being silly about this whole thing. He had a busy day and just forgot to call. There's no harm in that. In fact, I think I'll do a little Christmas shopping when I leave here."

At the moment I spoke those words, the Lord began to minister to me, "Go home!"

I didn't obey immediately. I tried to bargain with God. "Lord, I'm just going to run into Marshall's and T.J. Maxx for a quick minute. I won't really shop, just browse."

Immediately, the Lord sternly repeated, "Go home! Don't regret not going home!" The voice was so clear I *knew* I had to obey.

Suddenly I began to feel heaviness. When I got in the car, I called Joe again. This time I left a frantic message.

"Honey, please call me! I haven't heard from you all day. I'm on my way home. Please call me in the car." Fifteen minutes passed, still no call. I then called his sister, Ruth. Thank God, she picked up!

"Ruth? Have you heard from Joe today?" I anxiously asked.

"Yes," she said. "He called earlier this morning and said he had some work to do in the yard. He promised to come and see Momma later in the day, but I haven't seen or heard from him. Is anything wrong?"

"I don't know," I responded. "I'll have to call you back." I hung up the phone before she could ask any more questions. I began to pray. Uncontrollable tears streamed down my face. The drive home to College Park was about 40 minutes. Traveling around Interstate 285 West, I heard the voice of God comforting me. I cited all the Scriptures I could think of, Psalms 23 and 91. I rebuked the enemy with words of faith. I spoke the word of protection over Joe and against my own fear of the unknown. I stood on the promises of God. As I was praying, rain began pouring down. Driving became slower because of the heavy rain. I desperately wanted to get home in a hurry. I just kept praying and never stopped believing that everything would be okay.

In the midst of the heavy rain and the streams of tears on my face, I got a vision of my husband in distress near some steps. The steps looked like our hallway steps. My spirit told me Joe was in trouble, and I asked the Lord to let me get home before our 16-year old son, Ken. I didn't want Ken to find Joe lying there. I couldn't get home fast enough. I felt so helpless. I felt like my world had been suspended in time.

"Oh Lord," I cried. "Let me get home to Joe!"

My heart began to pound. I felt an immense loss, but I clung to the hope that Joe would pull through. Even though I continued to recite Scriptures, I didn't experience the peace I so desperately needed. In the spirit, I heard a *loud* piercing voice of distress and pain. I knew it was Joe.

"Hang on baby," I pleaded. "Hang on. I'm coming. I'm almost there."

My body convulsed with uncontrollable tears. Then a still small voice spoke to my heart.

"He's gone."

"Oh, Jesus No!" I cried. "Oh, Jesus No! You can't do this to me!"

My phone rang and this time the same piercing voice I had

heard earlier in my spirit was now real and coming from our 16 year old son, Ken.

"Mom, Dad is down on the ground and he's not responding! Where are you, Mom? Why isn't he answering me? Dad, wake up! Wake up, Dad! Mom, what am I supposed to do? He's not waking up." With each word, the shrill in his voice became louder and louder. "Mom, please hurry! Please hurry!"

"Son, I'm on my way. Right now, I need you to help me. Can you do that?"

"Yes, Ma'am."

My heart felt like it had been ripped away, but I had to be strong for Ken. I had to calm him down until I could get there. "Ken, I need you to call 911."

"I already have."

"Good," I said calmly. The tears were just a mere trickle now. "I'm here at our exit. I'm three minutes away."

After consoling him for a few more seconds, I asked him to call 911 again. "Son, stay on the phone with them until I get home. Will you do that for me?"

"Yes, Ma'am."

I called Clyde, my girlfriend Marian's husband, and asked him to meet me at the house. I explained that Joe had fallen on the steps and was not responding to Ken.

I got home at 5:05 P.M. and Ken was outside on the steps on the telephone talking to the 911 operator. I immediately got out of the car and rushed to Joe's side. He was lying face up on the landing near our front door. Instinctively, I knelt down to administer CPR, but he was cold to the touch. *He is gone,* I thought. I began to rub his face. The tears began again as pain washed over me. Everything else ceased to exist at that moment. I couldn't hear the sound of cars passing on the wet street. I couldn't hear Ken asking me if Dad would be okay. It was just Joe and me.

"Why did you leave me?" I pleaded through the tears. "Why? I love you so much. Don't leave me here alone! Joe, what am I going to do without you? No! No!"

The next thing I remember, paramedics were leading me into the house. Ken was still asking me about Dad.

"Is he going to be okay?" he asked. His eyes filled with confusion and fear.

"I'm not sure," I responded. "The paramedics are working on him to see what they can do. He may not make it." I grabbed the phone to call Joe's cousin, Rev. Horace Fuller, Jr. I needed someone to come and help me! He was a mentor and spiritual father, not to mention a strong right hand in a family crisis.

"Horace," I said. "Come to the house quickly. Something has happened to Joe. He's unconscious. The paramedics are working on him."

"Mamie, I'm on my way."

After thinking a minute, I quickly called back to Horace's house and spoke with his daughter Linda. I told her Joe was gone, but I didn't want the members of his church to know yet until I could tell his mother and sister.

A few minutes later, one of the medics solemnly entered into the hallway where I stood. "Ma'am, I am so sorry about your loss," he said quietly.

Yes, I knew, but it wasn't until that moment that those

words felt real to me. The paramedic did the best he could to console me, but all I could think of was, "Why did he have to say it? Why?" I felt a tinge of anger. I wanted the paramedics out of my house. I needed to call my family.

"Is Dad gone?" Ken asked.

I was in a daze.

"Mom, is Dad gone?" he repeated.

I shook my head.

"Tell me the truth. Is he gone?"

"Yes. Yes, baby. Dad is gone."

We embraced and cried. We held onto each other for dear life. I felt my knees giving way, but I didn't want to let Ken go. He broke away from me and rolled on the floor crying uncontrollably. My heart ached.

"Lord, what happened to my daddy?" he cried. "What are we going to do?"

While he cried, I prayed, asking God to give me strength, wisdom, and direction. Maybe this was just a dream. But no, it was *real*. The police had arrived and we were waiting for the coroner. I felt as though I was standing outside of myself. My tears had been spent and I needed to do something, *anything* to keep moving. *There was no time for grief,* I thought. I stepped outside. Joe was lying face up on the steps, his eyes and mouth closed, as if he were taking a nap.

The doormat had been placed on the shrubs. The mop, pail, scrub brush, and water hose were beside him. It had always been Joe's routine to sweep and clean the front porch after working in the yard. While I stood there, a slow drizzling rain began to come down. I hated the thought of Joe lying there uncovered on the steps. I went inside, got a blanket and covered him.

Afterwards, I called my friends Linda Carr and Bertha Davis. "Please come to the house, quick!" I said. "Something has happened to Joe." Linda called her husband Carnell and asked him to meet her there. Before they arrived, I got an umbrella and stood over Joe, protecting him from the rain. All the while, I tried to protect Ken and keep him away from the sight. When Linda and Bertha arrived and realized that Joe was dead, they took charge answering phone calls and trying to help me any way they could.

Clyde came, and shortly afterwards, Carnell arrived. I handed one of them the umbrella while I comforted Ken. By then, the rain had begun to pour and Joe was being dowsed with rain, but there was nothing I could do. The paramedics had said he couldn't be moved until the coroner had examined him. I felt so helpless, but I *had* to do something. I had to keep Joe dry. I asked Ken to help me gather more blankets to cover his father.

A swell of grief rose within me, but I suppressed it. Ken was scheduled to perform as a featured soloist at his school's Christmas concert in an hour. In my mind, I was trying to sort things out. At that moment, I looked up and Ken was standing before me.

"Mom," he said, "I have to go and sing at the concert."

I knew it was important to him, since he had worked so hard to have this opportunity. I considered stopping him from going, but decided against it. He looked at me and said, "Mom, I have to go because this is what Dad would have wanted." At that moment, I saw the depth of Ken's faith. You teach your children to trust God, but in difficult times, they prove how much they really trust Him for themselves. With that in mind, I let Ken go to the concert. I asked Clyde to take Ken to the school and to pick him up when the concert was over. Being sensitive to the situation, Clyde guided him through the garage to shield him from the possibility of seeing his father's body on the steps.

It seemed like an eternity, but the coroner finally arrived and pronounced Joe dead. I stood close by and watched every move he made as he examined Joe's ears, nose, mouth, throat, head and chest.

"Well?" I asked. "What happened?"

"Well, Ma'am. I won't know for sure until we do an autopsy, but it looks as though he has been here for several hours."

For some reason, I couldn't accept that answer. I called our family physician, Dr. Victoria, and told him what had happened. He was shocked because he had just seen Joe two weeks before and had given him his annual physical. Joe had been doing really well after having open-heart surgery 14 years earlier. In fact, Doctor Victoria had given him a clean bill of health. After conversing with Doctor Victoria, the coroner decided there would be no autopsy. He couldn't tell me at the time, but Joe had had a massive heart attack, had fallen backwards and had died in seconds.

The rain had stopped and the coroner respectfully placed a sheet over Joe. Friends helped to lift him on to the gurney and by 8:00 P.M. the paramedics, the coroner, and Joe were gone. Somehow, having Joe's body there gave me some comfort. Now, he was gone.

By this time, the telephone was ringing off the hook and I was feeling overwhelmed. I didn't know what to say to everyone. I had to contact our other children. Before I could make the calls people began to arrive. The Patricks, our neighbors from across the street, had seen the commotion and rushed over. Other friends showed up the moment they heard. Before long, the house was full of people. Somehow, the word had gotten out all over Griffin, which is where Joe pastored, and people had started making their way to our house.

As they arrived, I immediately put them all to work. I assigned Johnny Hunter, our godson, to answer the phone and take messages. I asked Anita McClain, my goddaughter, to take my telephone directory and begin making phone calls to notify close family and friends of Joe's death. My assignment was to find a way to break the news to our children, Larry, Greg, Sonya and Tina, Joe's 85-year-old mother, his sister, Ruth, and his twin sister Joann who lived in Charlotte, North Carolina. Although I didn't know exactly what I would say, I trusted God to guide me step-by-step. I just had to deliver the news before anybody else did. Word travels fast in close church communities like ours. Soon, cousins, uncles and aunts had heard. Immediately I thought, *how can I reach my children before they hear from someone else?* I thought about our daughter, Sonya, who has two young boys. I called her mother-in-law and asked her to take care of the boys. I called Robert, Sonya's husband.

I explained to him, "Tell Sonya that her father is in critical condition and might not make it. Bring her to the house right away." This may not have been the way someone else might have handled it, but as their mother, I would have done

11

anything to avoid causing my children pain.

When Robert arrived with Sonya, I told her that her dad was gone. At the very least, I thought Robert was there to console her, but later found out that on the way over he told her, "Your dad has been in an accident and he's gone to be with Jesus." I needed to contact Greg, Tina, and Larry before someone else got to them first.

I called Tina. She was a professor at Bowling Green State College at the time. I asked her department chair to send someone to be there with her when we called. When I was able to speak to her myself, I nearly broke down as I told Tina that her dad had had a massive heart attack and wasn't expected to live. I just couldn't bear telling her the truth when she was away from home. She never had the chance to say goodbye. I could scarcely believe that he was gone myself, and now I had to tell my children that they would never have the chance to talk with him, laugh with him, or even just say, "I love you, Dad." The thought of that overwhelmed me with such grief. I had to shield them. I had to protect them from the pain I felt for as long as I could.

"Tina," I said. "I need you to get on a plane as fast as you can. We don't know how long he'll be with us."

"Mama," Tina said between sobs. "Don't let him die. He can't die. Oh, Lord, please don't let him die..." The phone went silent. I heard muffled screams in the background. "Tina! Tina!" I screamed. "Pick up the phone!" After a few seconds, someone else picked up the phone and said, "Mrs. Harris?" I replied, "Yes."

"I'm Tina's friend Laura. Tina's okay. She's crying. She told me the news and I'm so sorry. Another friend of ours is here and is with her now. Is there anything I can do to help?"

"Yes, yes," I said urgently. "Please get her on the next plane to Atlanta."

"Yes, ma'am. I'll make sure. I'm so sorry about your husband. We'll pray that he'll pull through."

Those words sliced through my heart like a knife. It wasn't Laura's fault. She didn't know that Joe was already gone. However, the hope in her voice almost tempted me to believe that he was still with us and that this was all a horrible dream.

My next call was to my stepson, Larry. I can't really remember how the conversation went because my worst fear came true.

I said, "Larry, this is Mamie. "Something has happened to your dad. He had a massive heart attack and...."

"Yeah....yeah," he stammered. "Um, my mother just called and told me. My dad is dead!" I couldn't believe that someone else had already called him.

"I'm sorry, Larry," I confided. "I did my best to call you first. I didn't want you to find out like this."

After a pause that seemed like minutes, Larry said, "It's alright. I've got to call work and stuff, but I'll be there as soon as I can."

"That'll be good son," I said. "I'll see you soon...." Beyond that, I can't recall another word. Despite his concessions, I still felt that I had failed Larry for not reaching him before others did.

After talking to Larry, I called our son, Greg, in Miami, Florida. He was the most difficult to locate. As an Air Traffic

Controller, he worked odd hours. When I called the control center, one of his coworkers found him. I talked with Greg about an hour later.

"Greg, it's Mom. Dad had a massive heart attack." By now, I was getting weary from retelling the story. The fatigue from the day was setting in, but I *had* to tell the children, so I pressed on.

"How bad is it? Is he going to make it?" Greg asked.

"They don't think so, son." Something in my voice broke as the words passed my lips.

"Mom, Is he gone?"

I had no choice but to tell the truth. Greg has always been a perceptive child. He knows when something is wrong even before you tell him.

"Yes, Greg. Dad has left us."

"Oh, no Mom," he whispered. "I can't believe he's gone. Are you okay? Have you told everyone? Do you need me to call Tina, Sonya or Larry? How's Ken doing?"

"Yes. I've called all the children," I explained. "But I couldn't tell the girls like I did you boys. They are Daddy's little girls and I just couldn't tell them directly the way I did you."

"Mom," he interrupted. "What did you tell them?"

"I just said that Dad had a heart attack and wasn't expected to make it. With Tina away in Ohio and Sonya being close to Dad, I just didn't want to tell them over the phone. Thank God, Robert was able to bring Sonya over. We broke the news together. She's okay now. Sonya's a strong girl and so is Tina. They'll be alright...We'll be alright."

"You're right, Mom," Greg said. "We're going to be okay.

I'm just in shock right *now*. I can't believe he's gone. I just talked to him yesterday."

"I know son."

"Man. I just... I just can't believe it...."

"I understand. How soon do you think you can get here?"

"I'll be on the next flight out."

In addition to calling the children, there were so many other calls to make. Someone had to break the news to Joe's mom, his sister Ruth, my goddaughters Donna and Nicole, Joe's twin sister, Joann, and my best friend Alma. Finally, I had talked to everyone except his mother and his sister Ruth. By now, the house was buzzing with family, friends, members of our congregation, and Joe's sons in the ministry.

Many of the women brought food and offered to help in any way they could. Even with all the condolences and those tender touches on the shoulder, I felt alone. My husband was gone. I couldn't shake the numb feeling in my hands and my heart. It seemed there was no life in me. I felt empty. But, I thought, *all these people need me. My children need me. I need to be strong for them.*

I escaped to the bathroom for a moment alone. While smoothing my hair and staring at my reflection in the mirror with tears in my eyes, I couldn't help but think, *Get yourself together Mamie. All these people are here. You've got to keep it together. You've got to be strong.* Then I prayed, 'Lord, help me to glorify You. Give me the strength to let my light shine. Help me to be a living testimony of who You are in our lives."

It wasn't long before I felt obligated to rejoin my guests. I didn't want them looking for me or seeing me cry, so I quickly washed my face, took a deep breath and prepared myself to get back out there. However, as I turned the doorknob, grief gripped me. It enveloped me so tightly that I almost lost my breath. "Oh Lord," I cried. "What am I supposed to do? Where do I go from here? I've lost my husband, my children's father, my best friend. I woke up this morning with my husband in my arms and now he's gone. Yes, I know he's with you, Jesus, and I know I should be happy about that. Lord, I miss him. I miss him already. What am I going to do without him? How am I going to live without Joe?"

After Ken returned home from the concert, he greeted and comforted all the people. I saw strength in the way he shared his story with them. Joann, Joe's twin sister and her daughter Ingrid arrived in the early morning. Joann began asking about every detail surrounding Joe's death. She wanted to know if he said anything before he died. She asked what he was wearing, and what he was doing, etc. Finally, she got down on her knees facing Ken and they began holding hands, swaying back and forth, as Ken repeated the story to her. He suddenly stopped and said, "Aunt Joann, listen to me. He never said a word. He was on the steps asleep when I got here. He never woke up. You have to get yourself together."

TO GOD'S GLORY

Family and friends were still gathered in the house. After seeking solace in the bathroom for a few minutes, I knew I had to go back out and face them. I got myself together and walked out of the bathroom. Nevertheless, painful thoughts still flooded my mind as I wondered, *Lord, What am I supposed to say to all these people?* The Lord then reminded me that He'll never leave me or forsake me. (Joshua 1:5) That was such a comfort to me because I was feeling so down.

As I tried to encourage myself, I remembered what Joe always said when he talked about my being without him one day. He'd say, "You're a good woman, Mamie, and you'll know what to do when it's time. No matter what happens to me, I know you and the children will be fine." He had such confidence in me. Joe saw more in me than I saw in myself. He was such a man of integrity, one who truly loved and respected the Lord. He went the extra mile to mentor young ministers, and even though I was his wife, he always challenged me to be a better person. His words of encouragement are still with me today. There isn't a day that goes by that I don't think of him and the faith he had in me. The years we spent together, the conversations we had, and the problems we conquered together continue to encourage and motivate me.

It helps sometimes to keep the vision before you during times of trouble. Even though Jesus said "Let the dead bury the dead," I don't believe He was being insensitive. (Matthew 8:22) He doesn't want grief to keep us from giving Him glory. If we keep our mind on Him, He'll comfort us and show us what to do. That might sound like something "religious" people say, but I'm a witness of how true it is. Every time I got into the flesh, I felt unsure and helpless. But when I yielded to the comfort of the Holy Spirit, I knew with confidence that everything was going to be all right. I walked back toward the people with the Lord's Word resounding in me, I felt myself being transformed into a woman who had faith in God, a woman whose love for Joe would give God glory, a confident woman who knew what to do next.

I had to be sure that all of Joe's close family members had been contacted. I still had to notify Joe's mother, Rebecca, and his sister, Ruth. I had asked Rev. Horace Fuller, Jr., Joe's cousin, and Otis Willis, Jr., his best friend from his childhood, to go over and be there when I called so they could help them deal with the news of Joe's death. I didn't want them to be alone when they heard the news. However, before I could call his sister Ruth, Opal Lee, her sister-in-law who lived next door, had told her that Joe was dead. When Ruth heard the news, both she and Opal Lee responded with emotional outbursts that caused Joe's mother, to ask, "What's wrong?" They replied, "Joe is dead!" Grandma Rebecca was so overcome by shock and grief that she had to be sedated and put to bed.

The night ended with many of Joe's close family members arriving. Each one wanted to know exactly what had happened. I had told the story many times and really felt numb from the day's experience and the sheer unbelief of what had happened. I couldn't talk about Joe's death anymore, however, since most of the closest family members were there, we immediately began making funeral arrangements.

Early the next day, when I was trying to focus on how to prepare the program, Dr. Bill Scarborough, a local pastor and principal of the Montessori school where Ken had been a student called.

"I'm so sorry, Mamie," he said. "Is there anything I can do?"

"I have so much to do I don't know where to start", I responded. We didn't talk about the work that was ahead of me, but we talked about Joe, the funny things he did; the laughs we all had. It wasn't long after our talk that Dr. Scarborough arrived to help in any way he could. Talking to him was significant, as he was able to help me through the tougher times that came later.

I sat with Dr. Scarborough in the living room and outlined a tentative program for the funeral service. My primary goal was to give glory to God. I didn't want to offend anyone by not following the traditional order of service in the Baptist Church, but I really wanted it to be about Joe, his life and his service to the Lord. Dr. Scarborough guided me through the process and held my hand as I prepared the list of people to call. Planning Joe's home going celebration was one of the greatest challenges I had to face. I agonized over *who* should speak and in what order. Joe's family had come from a long line of pastors. We had spent our lives in ministry and I had learned how sensitive a time like this could be, not only for the immediate family, but for the congregation as well.

Dr. Scarborough asked, "Who do you want to speak?"

"I just don't know, Dr. Scarborough," I said. "There are so many people who will want to speak. We would be at the service until the next morning if I made room for them all."

He laughed and said, "Mamie, what do *you* want? Forget about the pressure for a moment and let the Spirit tell you who to call." With his words still ringing in my ears, I walked into the kitchen and stared at the bulletin board. My eyes rested on the telephone number of one of Joe's best friends, Jim Butler. We had lost contact with him over the years, but recently re-connected with him and his family. Joe had married Jim and his wife, Earlene in 1995. Ironically, we had received a Christmas card a few days earlier and Joe had asked me to get Butler's telephone number so he could give him a call. Just three days before, I had overheard them joking and laughing over the telephone. They talked for what seemed like hours. As I reflected on their rekindled friendship, I thought, *how could I call and tell him that Joe is gone now, when I can hardly believe it myself?*

God alone knows what I did to cushion each person that we had to contact. It wasn't easy, but the Scripture "I can do all things through Christ who strengthens me (Philippians 4:13) came to mind every time I felt unsure. After talking with

Butler, I began to remember many other military friends: A.J. Henderson in Pensacola, Florida, Marty Erwin in Norfolk, Virginia, and several others to whom Joe had been close. When you have a military career that spans 20 years, you meet many people along the way. As I called each one, I began to feel less anxiety. *This is the kind of home going Joe would want,* I thought to myself. He would want to be surrounded by family and those who knew him best.

While I was calling family and friends to tell them of Joe's passing, many calls were coming in. There were calls from people we had not heard from in years, yet they seemed to want the details of what happened. Some asked, "What can we do to help?" I wondered about their sincerity since they had not contacted us for years. I didn't feel that I needed to explain to them the details of our painful loss. Eventually, I had to decide not to talk to everyone who called. I asked a group of dedicated women from the church to screen the calls for me so that I could stay focused on what God would have me do and not what others thought would be best.

I contacted McDowell Funeral home in Griffin. Joe had often spoken well of the McDowells. He said they were Christian people who were very professional and efficient. They had told Joe how much they enjoyed his messages. My experience with them confirmed Joe's statements. They showed great compassion for the family. No matter what questions I asked, they went beyond the call of duty to serve me with the best they had to offer.

We scheduled the service for Tuesday, December 17, 1996 at Joe's home church at 1 P.M. Joe would be buried at

Westwood Gardens in Griffin with full military honors. The children and I chose everything, from the casket and flowers to what Joe would wear.

With the funeral arrangements made, I redirected my attention of the funeral service. I asked Bishop Kenneth Fuller to preside. He was not only Joe's cousin, but he was also the first of the sons in ministry that Pastor Harris had licensed and ordained. Pastor Harris' other sons were asked to be honorary pallbearers. But the question remained, "Who would deliver the home going message?" After all, we were without a pastor. The decision weighed heavily on me. But as the Lord directed me on how to set up the program, I knew that God would be glorified. My mind went back to a minister who preached on special occasions. There was no doubt that Reverend Dr. Cleopatrick Lacy, a local pastor and family friend, would be the most fitting person for the job. He had preached at my ordination in May of 1996 and for our 17th anniversary in ministry in November of the same year. He was a respected man of God who knew the family well and preached the truth without reservation. I knew that he would serve us well.

As God allowed the vision for the service to unfold, I called a friend to do a special flower arrangement for me. I sketched out a spread of red carnations shaped into the word "love" surrounded by a bed of white carnations. To some it may have appeared extravagant, but everything I did had a deeper meaning behind it. The red carnations represented the cleansing power in the blood of Jesus and the white represented purity and holiness. Many may not have understood, but I was committed to being obedient to the Lord and to what He had shown me.

Even in Joe's death, God would be glorified. This was truly a test for me. Now was the time to apply all of the things I had been taught about the Lord and His Word. I had been called to walk in love with everyone, even when I was physically and emotionally exhausted. People were tugging at me from every side. I know I got short with them a few times, which I regret. It was a difficult time. Looking back, I know I may not have explained what I was doing in a way that others understood. I just wanted to complete God's assignment.

As I sought the Lord, He began to bring to my mind certain people who should be added to the program. First, he helped me outline it. That's how God reveals things to me. As He said in His Word, "Write the vision and make it plain." (Habakkuk 2:2.) I sat at the computer and as I began to type out the program, the vision came to life. The Lord reminded me that Joe was in some ways like David, who was a man after God's own heart. Joe reverenced and honored God with a humble heart. Since it was a home going celebration, a black hearse didn't seem appropriate. We wanted to celebrate Joe's life and his going to be with the Lord! I immediately got on the phone and placed an order for a white hearse and white limousine for the processional. I also contacted a local rental company to set up a screen and camera to record the service and provide space in an overflow room so that friends who might not get to be seated in the main sanctuary could view the service.

The Lord also ministered to me concerning the way the family should enter the church. It was my experience that families grieve even more when the casket is opened. Many families in this situation don't want to witness every expression of grief as the body of their loved one lies before them. The Lord told me that it would be easier for us to come in last. It would allow some time for us to get our emotions together. Despite the pain we were going through, some still criticized the decision. I heard harsh statements of insensitivity, selfishness, and pride. It was obvious that they did not understand what God was doing. Much of what they said hurt me deep inside. I respected and trusted some of these people, yet they chose to say hurtful things. I had no idea that they had felt this way about me. I felt alone and misunderstood, but I trudged on. The Lord was going to be glorified, no matter what!

On Saturday before the Tuesday service, the family met for the first viewing. Joe looked great! He seemed to be asleep and at peace. He looked so well that I had to smile at this handsome fellow with his dashing good looks. Out of respect for the Deacons and the members of the congregation, I gave them the next opportunity to view the body before we opened viewing to the public. The Deacons were invited early Sunday morning for a private viewing and the church members were invited to view Joe after the morning worship service.

As the Deacons viewed the body, I gave them words of encouragement and prayed with them.

"Pastor Harris would want us to move on in the things of God," I said. I saw pain in some of their faces. All I could think to do was comfort them. As their First Lady, I wanted to be strong for them. "You have been charged with a great responsibility," I continued. "Each one of you has been equipped to stand in the gap for your brothers and sisters in the absence of your Shepherd. Encourage one another as I have with you this morning. Comfort the congregation and love them as Pastor Harris loved you." I prayed with them once more. Without hesitation, I believed they would stand in faith to be a light to the rest of the congregation. When the members arrived, for the viewing, our family greeted and comforted each of them as they paid their respects to Pastor Harris. These were very trying times for all of us. We cried together and held each other for strength.

After the viewing, we all headed home. All of the children were there. Being together provided some comfort, but as we approached our home, all the chattering gradually began to taper-off. None of us said it, but I knew what was happening. We all dreaded coming back to our home knowing that Joe was no longer there. We were all running full speed ahead and we had not had time to rest. My body began to cry out emotionally and physically. There were many times when I just wanted to find a quiet place to sleep and cry. But every time I tried, someone needed me or there was always some place I needed to be. Needless to say, the bathroom became my favorite hiding place. I couldn't stay too long, however, before someone would ask, "Are you okay?" I know everyone meant well, but I just didn't get a chance to sort through my grief alone.

Being a private person, I needed time to myself to process what was going on and what I needed to do next. I didn't want to be rude, so I hid my grief rather than let everyone see it. Unfortunately, through my example, I taught my children to do the same. I showed them that everyone depended on us to be strong. Instead of giving the burden to God, I took it up by trying to meet everyone's needs and ignoring my own. I know

now that a dry vessel will break when new wine is poured into it. (Matthew 9:17) I needed refreshing, but after all the criticism I had been getting and the fact that I was used to leading people, I felt that I couldn't show my vulnerability to anyone.

The night before the funeral, I cried out to God in the wee hours and asked Him to carry me through this wilderness experience. He comforted me and provided what I needed at the time. Just as He promised in Proverbs 3:24, He gave me sweet rest. I had not rested that well in days. I woke up on the morning of the funeral refreshed, though sad. I missed waking up to Joe and I didn't want to say goodbye for now.

Shortly after we awakened, we had to start getting ready for the service. It wouldn't be long before the car would arrive to take us to the church. One of my devoted sisters in the Lord prepared breakfast for the family, but I couldn't eat much. I said a few things to the children, but none of us felt like talking. I knew I would see Joe again, but that didn't stop me from missing his presence, the curves in his face and the tone of his voice. I walked back into the room I had shared with him, and my eyes began to well up again. I thought about how many years we had spent together. I hardly knew who I was without him.

As always, the Lord picked me up and carried me through the service. When it was over, I knew it was the Lord who gave me the strength to press on. I didn't realize how closely people were watching me at the time. Later, some commented, "I don't see how you're able to cope so well. You're so strong. Your husband just went home to be with the Lord and you're still supporting others in their time of grief."

While these words appeared to offer encouragement and admiration, others weren't so kind. Some said I wasn't grieving enough. I guess they wanted to see more emotion. In fact, one woman was quoted as saying, "She's taking it so casually. If she really loved him, she would have at least shed a few tears." What they didn't know was that God's grace and mercy had carried me through the valley of the shadow of death. I couldn't have gone through losing my husband so suddenly if the Holy Spirit, the Comforter, had not been with me. I wondered why Christians could not comprehend this.

Thinking back, I wonder if my words of encouragement and tribute to Joe at the service caused people to misunderstand me. At Joe's home going service, I gave words of exhortation and encouragement to the many pastors and members. I talked about Joe's commitment to his calling, how those of us left still had work to do for the Kingdom, and how we had to continue his vision. What they didn't realize was that I was operating in a daze, speaking well and impressing people with my calmness and strength, while I quietly lamented in my heart.

After the home going celebration was over, I was at home alone. The children hadn't arrived yet because they were still with friends trying to cope with the finality of the day. I knew that they didn't want to come home. Nothing was the same and it never would be. Just like my heart, the house felt so empty and alone. I closed my eyes, trying to drown out the voice of silence.

I thought back over the days before Joe's death and wondered if I could have said or done something to prevent his death. I wondered if I had known that night would be our last night together, would I have said or done something differently? I couldn't be sure what I would have done. Only God knows.

On the night before Joe's death, we had discussed putting our house on the market in February of the next year. We had discussed plans to move into a ranch style house, a house without steps since we were getting older. All of our children were gone except for Ken, and he would graduate within two years. This had been an ongoing discussion for a while, but I wondered if Joe really wanted to move. He had agreed that we would move, but he made no plans to move forward with the idea. He'd told our daughter Sonya earlier in the week, "I'm not sure if I want to move or not. I'd just as soon go to glory from here." Ironically, that was exactly what had happened.

This experience confirmed what the Word says about the words of our mouths. Life and death, blessings and curses are in the power of the tongue (James 3:9). As I thought back on the situation, it seemed like a self-fulfilling prophecy. I realized we had not been on one accord about the move. After all, when Joe reluctantly agreed to look for another house, I knew he had not settled the issue in his spirit. I thought, "Did our discussion cause him stress? Could I have prevented his heart attack? I felt tremendous grief and a heavy weight on my shoulders. I needed rest. I couldn't think about the situation one more minute. I began to recite Psalm 91. It comforted me as the Lord quietly lulled me to sleep.

I woke up early to the same deafening silence I'd experienced the night before. My hand instinctively reached over to Joe's side only to find it empty and cold. It was almost as though I had forgotten the last few days, only for my heart to be jolted back into reality. As my eyes opened, I began to think, *Where are all the people?* I was so used to all the activity that its absence was unfamiliar to me. I got up and walked to the kitchen.

It was 9:00 A.M. I must have been exhausted. As the day wore on, I only received a handful of phone calls from friends to see how I was doing. Surprisingly, none of the people who had been filling my home for the past few days reached out to me. It wasn't long before I realized that I had to face this loss alone. *Joseph is gone! Joe is gone. My honey is gone. I am a widow.* I kept saying these words to myself over and over again. Each time I thought these words, the reality became clearer. I was now a widow with a young son who no longer had a father. Suddenly, I felt powerless and alone. My eyes welled up with so many tears that my entire being was drenched with sorrow. *Why am I still crying?* I thought. I realize now that those tears were medicine to me. They brought healing to my broken heart.

My understanding of the Word helped me to believe that the church would take care of Ken and me. The Bible commanded the church to support widows and orphans, and that truth brought comfort to me. I truly believed that the Deacons and the church would help me through the difficult transition ahead.

Joe's unexpected death made it difficult for me to return to work. I had a few bereavement days, but had exhausted them previously when I took off because of my illness. Reality hit me again. I kept asking myself, *where do I go from here? How am I going to support my teenage son?"* I walked into Joe's office and grabbed his favorite Bible, the one with copious notes in the margins. It still had his scent. The Word of God was a constant comfort when I didn't know what to do or who to turn to. Regardless of what it looked like, I knew that God was leading and guiding my steps.

I went back to church the last Sunday of 1996. Walking through those doors without my husband and pastor was excruciatingly painful for me. I took each step by faith, believing that everything would be all right. I wasn't sure I was ready to return to the church, but I knew that my presence would strengthen the church family and would help us to weather the struggle together. I took my usual seat.

Many of the members asked how I was doing. I politely responded that the family was doing well. I knew they meant well, but I just couldn't help thinking, *why are you talking to me now? I haven't heard from most of you in weeks.* I didn't realize until much later that they were waiting for me to ask for help. I just assumed that the church *knew* what I needed and how alone I felt. I didn't think I had to ask. Handling things on my own was something I had been doing all my life. I didn't know how to be any other way. I was so used to helping others that I often forget to ask for help when I needed it. I hadn't had time to prepare mentally or emotionally for Joe's death. One minute I was showing him how to work the washer and a few hours later, he was gone. Everything in my life had changed forever and I wasn't sure how I should feel about it. One thing was for sure, I was emotionally weary and physically drained from the loneliness and grief that seemed to consume me.

After church service, Ken, Sonya and her children went

with me for our customary Sunday dinner with Joe's mother. At the dinner table, we all agreed to go ahead with plans to have dinner at my house for Christmas. Joe's sister and niece freely talked about how much they missed him and the loneliness they felt. Joe was their brother and uncle, but I was his *wife*. The only person I felt could relate to my pain was his mother. I had promised Joe long before he died that I would care for his mother in any way I could.

"Grandma Rebecca," I said. "It's me and you now. Like Ruth was with Naomi, I am committed to you no matter what. You don't ever have to worry because I promised Joe that I would take care of you. I know that Ruth is here for you, but I'll do my best to fill in for Joe."

"You know Mamie," she responded. "I don't know how I can live without Joe. He was one of the best children I had. He didn't mind doing anything in this world for me. You know, he was always different from the others. I just don't think I can live without Joe... my little preacher." My words of consolation meant very little to her. She loved Joe so much, and she loved everybody who loved him. She was so proud of how he had turned his life around and was living for the Lord. Sadly, losing a child was nothing new to Grandma Rebecca. She had already lost her fifth child, David, in September 1995 and James, her second born had died just three months earlier the same year. Now Joseph, her son from her first set of twins, was gone.

It nearly broke our hearts to watch Grandma Rebecca grieve her children and the loss of her last surviving brother a year earlier. Her heart was heavy with grief.

Her brother, Reverend Freeman Fuller, Sr., had passed

away from a massive heart attack while ministering at a local church. I am sure she felt anxiety and fear because she had endured a massive heart attack in 1985.

I empathized with Grandma Rebecca because I, too, had experienced a lot of grief lately. Joe's death came right on the heels of losing my mother in 1995 after a brief illness. Just like with Joe, I had little warning. One day she was feeling a bit under the weather, and the next week she was gone. I never thought I would fully recover from her sudden death and now this. I kept hoping that I would wake up and find that this was all a horrible dream.

Grandma Rebecca and I continued to share our common loss and talked about how each person had affected our lives. We shed tears together as we comforted each other. That Sunday afternoon I made up my mind that I would move to Griffin and be Grandma Rebecca's primary caregiver. When I shared my decision with her, she said, "Mamie, I don't want you to do that. You've got to take care of my baby Ken."

We talked by telephone and in person for the next few days. Then, on Monday, December 30, the next week, I received a frantic phone call from Joe's sister, Ruth. She had had to take Grandma Rebecca to the emergency room. The doctor examined her and sent her home, after diagnosing her with bronchitis. On Tuesday, she collapsed and was transported by ambulance to the emergency room again, where we learned that she had been misdiagnosed. She had pneumonia.

Ken, Tina, Sonya and I rushed to Griffin to see her. She was in such high spirits, laughing and talking. We left the hospital feeling relieved and thinking that she would recover.

On January 1, I received a message on the answering machine telling me that Grandma Rebecca was gone. I found out later they had connected her to the life support machine. I grabbed a few things just in case we needed to stay for a few days and Ken and I left for Griffin. All I could think was, *why is this happening Lord? First, Joe and now Grandma Rebecca.* It seemed as though death was all around me. I knew no other way to cope with everything except to pray.

As I drove to Griffin, I prayed for strength and for Grandma Rebecca's health. I knew that she was in her 80's and had to die eventually, but why so close to Joe's death? I cried out, "Where are you, Lord?" How much more can we take? Why is so much happening to us?" Speeding down the highway, glimpses of my life flashed before me. I saw all the people that had touched my life and were now gone. I thought of my mother, Joe and Grandma Rebecca. I then turned my thoughts to Ken, and the tremendous loss he had endured in such a short time. He was young to have experienced so much loss.

Suddenly, it sounded as if someone was calling me from a long distance away. I was jolted back to reality when I heard Ken calling out for me. I had been deep in thought trying to figure out all of the "what ifs." "Mom! Mom! "Do you think Grandma is going to make it?" he asked. I looked over toward him in the passenger seat. He looked so scared. My heart sank. I was torn between telling him the truth and sparing him more pain. "Ken," I said. "We'll pray that she'll wait until we can get there. However, we must understand that to be absent from the body is to be present with the Lord. Grandma is now on a machine and I'm sure it's very painful for her. I know you don't want her to be in pain. Let's keep the faith that she will recover." I then asked him to lead us in prayer about Grandma Rebecca. We eventually drifted back to our own thoughts, reflecting on the losses we'd already suffered and the dread of the unknown.

Just as I pulled into the hospital parking lot, Ken and I saw our family leaving through the double glass doors, with their heads hung in sorrow. Ken blurted out, "Oh no! Grandma's gone!" Richard, Joe's brother, came to the car and confirmed the worst. At this point, I had been through so much pain I couldn't cry anymore. Death was all around me and the shock of it was exhausting. Even our dog, Skipper, died that day. One by one, family came to the car giving us the details of what had happened. The doctor had already informed the family that there was little hope of Grandma Rebecca surviving this crisis. Since she was on life support, everyone had agreed to have the doctor unplug it. She had quietly slipped away. Somehow, none of us wanted to believe that she was gone. Whether we cried openly or not, we all felt an immense sense of grief.

Much to our disbelief, we were again sitting around the family dining table trying to plan another home going celebration. So much of our energy had been sapped out of each one of us that we barely had enough compassion to comfort one another. The pressure was getting to all of us. Some of us wanted to be left alone, while others found comfort in the company of the friends and relatives that came by to visit. Each of us had to find our way to grieve for our mother, sister, aunt and friend while trying to heal from Joe's death, too. It was not easy. It was the most painful experience of my life. One thing

I knew for sure: my patience to endure was being tested. As always, the family relied on me to take the lead in making the final arrangements. From the flowers to the service and burial, I made most of the arrangements alone. I had grown weary from making decisions, and supporting and comforting everyone else. *What about me?* I thought.

Having been in the Harris family all of my adult life, I had always been treated like a sister and a daughter. So, naturally when we all sat down together to make the funeral arrangements, it was like opening another wound. Tears began to flow as we greeted people, some of the same people we'd seen a couple of weeks earlier. We did our best to support one another, but there were times when I was impatient with people, especially my family. I felt so empty, yet everyone expected so much of me. I began to think, *no one really cares about me and how I'm dealing with all of this.* I know my feelings were not based on reality. There were many people sharing their love for me during that difficult time. Even still, because of my pain, I just couldn't receive what I needed from them. As the saying goes...Hindsight is 20/20 and I regret not leaning on my friends more. I kept many of my feelings inside. I realize that Satan was trying to trick me. He wanted me to get so down and depressed about Joe and Grandma Rebecca that I would doubt my belief in God. I praise the Lord for preserving me during that time. The enemy is *always* looking for someone he can devour. When you go through something as tragic as two deaths in a few weeks, if you are not careful, you can lose your confidence in God's Word and begin to doubt His promises.

As one would expect, Grandma Rebecca's home going

preparation did not go well. We were all so distracted by grief that we kept forgetting important details. We were all broken vessels trying to plan a home going celebration. Finally, we were able to get everything finalized on paper. After planning the service, we knew there were other things that had to be dealt with later. We needed to decide what to do with Grandma's house, and who would be the executor of her will? None of us could think of what to do at the time. The grief was just too great to bear. I thought, *if we could just get through the funeral, the rest would take care of itself.* However, the fact of the matter was that none of us was emotionally and mentally prepared to make those difficult decisions. Tough choices were on the horizon, ones that would change the course of my life and further test my trust in God.

THE CLOUD MOVES

The next few years following Joe's death proved to be the most challenging ever. I was still often in a fog, only functioning at about fifty percent, but trying mightily to operate as if I had control of the situation. There were days that I'd find myself wandering around in a shopping mall, at a gas station or a grocery store with tears streaming down my face. The smallest thing would trigger memories of Joe, the faint scent of his favorite cologne as someone walked past me, the sight of a man wearing his style of clothing, the sound of someone calling his name in a crowded food court, or simply my thoughts of how lonely I had become without him. Men's clothes in department stores reminded me that I had no reason to look for a matching shirt and tie to surprise Joe. Every day I felt like someone was sticking pins in my heart. I was being tortured and no immediate relief was in sight.

I had always considered myself a strong, independent

woman, but somehow through my years of marriage, I had come to depend on Joe. I had come to see myself in relation to him, his ministry and his goals. I didn't plan it; it just happened. My own dreams and aspirations were meshed with his, and my identity was undeniably linked to that of my husband. I was Pastor Harris' wife. I was Pastor Harris' executive administrator. I was considered the First Lady of the church my husband pastored, but who was I as a person? Now, I had to sort out who *Mamie* really was. I had to determine what my purpose was and how I would continue my life without Joe. I was the First Lady at 8 A.M. one day and by 5 P.M. the same day, I was the last lady! People began calling me Sister Harris. I realized that "First Lady" was associated with my husband Joe's position and not God's calling.

The major question became, what will be my role in the church? In addition, I had to figure out how my son and I would survive - not only emotionally, but also more importantly, financially. Where would the money come from to support my son, myself and our home? The reality of my financial situation hit me when Joe's retirement check was automatically deposited into our account and I realized I had to return it because he was deceased. I had enough faith in God to know that He would provide, but the question of *how* was always in the forefront of my mind. I knew it would take time for me and the family to heal emotionally from Joe and Grandma Rebecca's deaths.

With the loss of Joe as pastor of the church, I thought the first step was to make sure that the church had as smooth of a transition as possible and that the vision would live on.

Life had to take on some form of normalcy, but I didn't know where to begin. This became difficult to do, especially when every day I looked in the closet and saw Joe's clothes. Immediately, the wound would be reopened.

I began to ask myself, when would I let go, take off my grave clothes, and come forth as Lazarus did? I became so involved in helping the church members that my grieving process was suppressed. I just said, "I'll grieve later when we get a new pastor." The immediate need was for the congregation and the family to remain intact. We needed to protect all that we had worked to accomplish in the 17 years of our lives. We had made many sacrifices to achieve the goals we had set for the church. Because of my love for God and the church, I promised the Lord that I would do whatever I could to keep our church family together. In spite of my own grief, I would exhort, encourage and comfort those who needed it. I knew that God would be strong in my weakness. I also knew that the best way for me to get past Joe's death was to stay busy continuing the work he loved.

I asked the deacons if we could meet and come up with a plan of action to move forward. As Pastor Harris' widow, I wanted to discuss matters with them regarding my continued role in the church and other issues relative to retirement pay and provisions for our family. We met about two weeks after Joe's death.

Since I had been ordained as a minister in May of 1996, I offered to continue to serve the church in a leadership role, carrying out the order of service and helping the church transition through the selection of a new pastor. Most of the deacons seemed in favor of my serving in this capacity, but one very outspoken deacon said, "I wasn't in favor of you being ordained in the first place and I won't vote for you now!" In reply, I said, "Well, it's really not about me; it's about carrying on the vision of the church!" This deacon then replied, "As far as I'm concerned, when Pastor Harris died, the vision died with him!" At that moment, the pain and devastation of his words almost brought me to tears. It was as if he had stuck a knife straight through my heart! How could the deacon whom my husband had supported make such an unkind, cutting statement? Did he have *no* respect for me or for Joe? I was crushed by his response.

I thought of all the hours Joe had spent with the members of the church - marrying them, praying for them and their families, getting up in the middle of the night to bail their children out of jail, going to their homes at 2 o'clock A.M. after the death of a family member, and staying up long hours praying and pondering over sermons to make sure he was shepherding them as the Holy Spirit led. He often missed our children's baseball games; plays and other school activities because he was passionately committed to the church, its needs, the deacons and the members. It wasn't fair that our children had to share their father with the entire church when sometimes they needed him more. I thought of all the hours I had been without my husband when he did things for the church, allowing the ministry to take priority over our family life and even our personal relationship as husband and wife. How could this deacon sit there and say what he did? I could not understand how he could be so cruel. With no support from the other deacons, the meeting ended with the understanding that I would do what they asked of me and no more. I could not believe these were the spiritual leaders of the church. Already filled with pain, I was even more saddened by their rejection.

As far as finances were concerned, I had significant expenses. There was no offer from the church to help pay the cost of the funeral, burial or anything else, so I had to pay for Joe's funeral from family funds. It was also the Christmas season and I knew our regular monthly bills would soon arrive. I was not earning money from my job, since I had had to take time off without pay to prepare for Joe's funeral and to recover from the shock of the whole situation. I asked the deacons what money I would get from the church. They indicated that there was no retirement fund or widow's benefits, but they gave me Joe's salary for the last week of December and agreed to give me half of my husband's salary for the month of January. After that, I was to no longer receive money from the church. Knowing that I had no significant income to rely on, I asked the Chairman of the Deacon Board if I could get the equivalent of a loan from the church until I could get on my feet. One deacon stated, "We'll get back with you." To this day, I have never heard a word from the deacons about my request. There was no proposal to help me and the family transition to our life without Joe. I felt abandoned by the very people my husband had poured his life into.

I eventually came to the hard realization that the church would not help me financially and I had to figure things out myself. I had always managed the finances, so it was not a problem for me to continue doing so. The real issue was in knowing from where the resources would come. There was no father or close family member I could turn to for guidance. I had to evaluate where we could go financially and juggle which bill to pay and which one would have to wait. I was so grateful that we had taken out life insurance policies on the car loans, which meant that they were paid in full upon receipt of the death certificate. I realized that I could only trust God to get me through the financial crisis. I had to develop a plan of action and stick to it.

After careful consideration, I prioritized my list of financial obligations, began closing out and changing accounts, and contacting utility companies. It all became so overwhelming. My flesh said, "You can't do this, but my spirit said, "You can do all things through Christ who strengthens you" (Philippians 4:13). I vowed not to make any major decisions right away, not even whether to sell the house or remain in it and endure the painful memories surrounding the sudden death of my husband. Every time I walked across the threshold of the door or pulled into the driveway, I would relive that horrible day. In my present mental condition, I knew that any decision made would not have been in my best interest. I longed for someone to come and rescue me! I wanted someone else to take care of these matters. Everyone was so sure that I had it all together that very few took the risk of asking, "Is there anything I can do to help you?" I wished Joe's best friend would come by and say something to the children and me, but he never did.

In the time leading up to Joe and Grandma Rebecca's death, I spent considerable time away from my job because I was bombarded with family situations. By the time Joe passed away, I had used all my vacation time. When my mother became suddenly ill in 1995, she was diagnosed with pancreatic cancer. I took time from work to deal with her surgery and death. It seemed that I was always the caretaker of the family, partly because I felt the need to be there and because others depended on me.

After Joe's funeral and the Christmas holidays had passed, I intended to return to work the first of the year. Unfortunately, Joe's mother passed on January 3, making it necessary to stay away from work longer. I was not in an emotional state to return to work. I just needed more time to recover. Some days I could not pull myself out of bed. At the time all the deaths took place, I repeatedly had trouble with my lower back. In the midst of all the emotional turmoil, I was frequently visiting the doctor to diagnose my ailment. He discovered I had two herniated disks, prescribed medication and told me I needed rest in order for my back to heal properly.

Although I provided my boss with appropriate doctor's statements documenting my health issues, she required that I return to work and sent me a series of letters to that affect. I was hurt that she did not understand nor did she seem at all sensitive to my emotional and physical pain. Finally, dreading it profusely, I returned to work in March of 1997. I was still suffering from back pain, but knew that I needed the money and needed to respond to my boss's requests or possibly be fired. At the time, I was employed with the Office of Personnel Management with a total of 18 years of service. I was a dedicated worker and faithful employee prior to these circumstances. It seemed as if I was given no compassion after years of committed service to the government.

Upon my return to work, my boss assigned me to the duties of a receptionist on the front desk where I had to answer several telephone lines that were constantly ringing. I was expected to meet and greet walk-in customers, explain information, accept applications and other documents, make referrals, and serve as the first point of contact for the office. At first, I understood that I would rotate through this assignment along with other employees, but I was later told that it was my permanent reassignment. This had not been my job when I left to attend to my husband's death. It seemed like retaliation for my being out of the office.

With the grief I still carried, I was subject to cry at any moment and had difficulty sitting at the desk for prolonged periods because of my back. I just could not continue to face people with tears and sadness hour after hour, day after day. Sometimes I would find myself crying at my desk. The wind was out of my sail. I was lifeless. It seemed like the whole world was against me. In many ways, I felt like Job. My mother had died suddenly. My husband had died of a massive heart attack. My mother-in-law had died. Our dog, Skipper, had died the same day of my mother-in-law's death. I had lost significant income. My children were distressed. I had back problems. I felt forced to leave my job. My home was unsettled, and I had no peace of mind. I knew God was there, because His Word says, (Hebrew 13:5) "I will never leave you nor forsake you," but I didn't feel His comfort nor see His intervention, as I would have liked. I wanted to be supernaturally lifted out of this painful situation. At that time, I did not know the full plan of God and what he was working out in my life.

One day while sitting at the front desk in pain, I cried out in my heart, "Lord, please help me! What am I going to do?" I heard Him reply, "Will you give up everything to follow me?" My heart was quickened because I knew that the Lord was telling me to leave this job and never look back. He wanted me to trust Him fully for my life, my finances, emotional and physical healing and even my calling to minister to others. He had tugged at my heart in the past to give up everything for the Kingdom and I had just held on, thinking there would be a better time than the present to step out on faith. This time, I knew that I *had* to obey. Therefore, I did. I resigned that very day and God has done exceedingly, abundantly above all that I could ever ask or think! (Ephesians 3:20) I have never lacked nor wanted for anything that the Lord has not provided. In fact, the remainder of Ken's private school tuition was paid by an anonymous donor. This act of kindness took a tremendous burden off me and demonstrated to me God's faithfulness.

In the midst of everything, I continued to support the church any way I could. The time leading up to finding and installing a new pastor was not easy. Our church was without a pastor for 11 months. Our faith was tested every day. All of us were wounded in one way or another. Out of our own pain, we wounded others and each other. Everything we did was filtered through our pain. I came to realize that emotions could lead you down the wrong path. That's why it's so important to pray constantly, especially when there are trials and tribulations in your life. Somehow, we muddled through those 11 months by the grace of God.

In November 1997, our new pastor was selected. We began making plans for his installation that was to be in February of 1998. Since I was asked to work on the installation committee, I thought my relationship and acceptance in the church was established. I had been the key person responsible for recruiting the new pastor and encouraging members to seek God about voting for him. I felt he was the man for the job. I believed he was a godly man who was led by the Holy Spirit. I thought he understood the Bible well enough that he would dispel the traditional Baptist view that women could not be preachers.

We spent several days working on the installation program, ensuring that the new pastor was welcomed with love and respect. The program was a tremendous success, and I felt that my administrative and ministry gifts were obvious. I hoped that my gifts would make room for me in the new pastor's regime. After the installation, everyone took his or her places in the ministry. Surprisingly, I was not given an assignment. While I felt that I could mentor the new pastor and his wife in ministry since they were young and I had so many years of ministry experience, they obviously did not see things the way I did.

When no place was made for me, I decided to talk with the pastor. I explained that my desire was to fulfill the call of God on my life. I knew without a doubt that God had called me to minister to the broken-hearted and set the captives free (Luke 4:18-19). I told him that I would assist with the outreach ministry until God gave him direction for the church. I let him know I would be willing to work with him in the ministry. He expressed his ideas about what a woman's role should be in the church. I was surprised to learn he had the same traditional

Baptist view that many others had. He couldn't see women in positions of authority over men. I was stunned and disappointed by his attitude. Again, I cried out to God, "Why Lord? Why am I being treated this way when I know you have called me to preach and teach?"

After many months passed and he never asked me to serve or ever got back to me regarding our conversation, I realized he was not interested in having me serve in ministry at this church. I was torn between staying at the church where I had been so comfortable for over 35 years and going out into the unknown.

My heart's desire was to remain in the church that my husband had pastored for 17 years. It was the church that my husband's grandfather had founded. All my family and friends were in this church. I began to think to myself, "Why isn't there a place for me?" After all, hadn't I been the First Lady and received the respect and consideration of the congregation as someone with an opinion that counted? I felt like I was being pushed out. I knew I had to go, but I had some fear and doubt. God, however, was ordering my steps. He knew what was ahead even though I did not. He just wanted me to trust him.

Still, I didn't leave right away; however, I found it especially hard to stay when the church family I loved so much and gave everything to, became my greatest critics. I saw the entire church give the new pastor their unwavering support. They supported the lucrative salary and benefits package for the new pastor that included retirement, life insurance and a paid vacation while they didn't show nearly the same level of sensitivity to my husband.

At the last annual conference, they failed to support a salary increase for Joe. It was as if Joe and I had been dismissed by our own home church. This was more than I could endure. I became bitter and angry. I'm sure my emotional response was triggered by anger at Joe's death and some bitterness and resentment at how the church gave no support to my dependent child and me, a widowed pastor's wife. We had invested so much, yet received so little. I knew I could no longer stay in this church. I was at the end of my rope, but where would I go? What would I do?

I began to question God, "God, who will be my pastor? What do you want me to do?" Before I could even pose these questions, I heard Him say, "Feed my sheep!" I asked him, "How and where do you want me to feed them? I can't stay here. I don't even know where I'm going."

After God spoke to my heart, I began having a fellowship at 8 o'clock A.M on Sunday mornings in the clubhouse of a local apartment building with my two children and three friends. I had started this fellowship during the time the church was searching for a pastor and they were bringing different ministers in to preach. Even though I had started this fellowship, I was still attending the regular 11 o'clock services at our home church, where I had been a member for over 30 years. Gradually, more and more people showed up at the fellowship. Even after the new pastor was installed, we continued the 8 A.M. service with a small group of faithful people and went to our home church for regular services. However, before too long, the fellowship began to grow and we had to find a new place to meet that would accommodate the people. I began to see God was working in the midst of our fellowship. I also came to the realization that I had to formally break my ties to the new pastor and our home church. It was apparent that the glory cloud had moved and I had no choice but to move with it. I followed the Lord.

What I've learned from all of the trials I encountered is that following the Lord is not as easy as we think. We often say we will give up everything to follow Him, but when the time comes, we have many excuses. We often have fears. We can look at the rich young ruler (Matthew 19: 16-22) and say we would not be like him. We say we would never let money or material things keep us from following the Lord. Eventually, the question will become, "Do we really mean it?" Will we *really* leave *everything* to do the will of the Lord? I have now settled that question in my mind and in my heart: "Yes, Lord. I *will* follow you!"

Another lesson I've learned is that many people fail to realize that God's chosen leaders are human and often have the same problems and concerns as everyone else; yet, they are required to minister to others. Ministers' wives have personalities, gifts and callings, and should be looked at not only as helpmates to their husbands, but also as individuals with their own place in the Kingdom. Despite their humanness, the minister's family is forced to live in a glass house, with everyone scrutinizing and criticizing their every move and decision. In the end, we all must realize that only God can judge. It's not our place to judge and condemn others.

My experience of losing my husband, leaving my job, and being rejected by the church brought a form of death on many levels. When my husband died, parts of me died with him. It was as if I died on one level spiritually and emotionally and was resurrected on another. Jesus said, "Truly I tell you, unless a kernel of wheat, falling into the ground, dies, it remains alone. But if it dies, it bears much fruit (John 12:24). I realized that I had to die ain order to live and do the will of my Father.

These death experiences were like the fire of the Holy Spirit burning impurities out of me, compelling me to be obedient to God's will in my life, to fulfill my purpose, my destiny. Like the Apostle Paul who had to become blind before he could see the truth of who Jesus Christ was (Acts 9), I had to have a death experience before I could live to do God's work. A pastor's family always lives under much scrutiny and is always subject to the approval of others, especially the church members. God caused a shift in my mindset and spirit. After coming through the fire, I no longer cared whether people thought I was called to be a minister or pastor. It didn't matter what they thought about me, my gifts and callings, or whether they validated me or not. I was free. I knew in my heart of hearts that the Lord had anointed me to preach good tidings to the meek; he had sent me to bind up the brokenhearted, to proclaim liberty to the captives, and open the prison to them that are bound. I had been set free. Now I could set others free.

I understand now that God was molding and shaping me for my assignment. He knew I could not guide others through a path that I had not come through myself. I was walking in my destiny - that place where God had brought me by lead-ing me through the valley of death and hell and allowing me to be resurrected as a living witness of new life in Christ.

Truly, I can testify as the Apostle Paul did, that, "…all things work together for good to them that love God, to them that are the called according to his purpose (Romans 8:28)." God has an expected end for me (Jeremiah 29:11) and it will be manifested in my life even through the hardships and challenges. The question for my life at that time which remains even today is "Can you come through the fire without the smell of smoke on your clothes?"

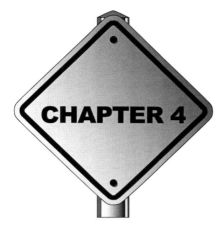

GOD'S LITTLE ACORN

Often times I think back on my life with Joe and remember where I came from and how God has always been a part of my life, guiding me when I made mistakes, giving me dreams and visions, and helping me achieve them when it would have been impossible without Him. It seems that my life was in danger many times, but in retrospect, I know it was the love, grace, and mercy of God that reached out and saved me over and over again. God always had a specific purpose for my life and He proves that time after time with His favor. From my early existence, the favor of God has been on my life much like that of Esther in the Bible who went before the king to save her people. In many areas of my life, God has allowed me to be a pioneer for others coming after me.

I am my mother's first child - born out of wedlock and raised by her and my stepfather, who was a sharecropper in Griffin, Spalding County, GA. Some of my fondest childhood memories are of church. We attended Bethel Grove Christian Methodist Episcopal Church on Jackson Road in Griffin. I have vivid memories of the 1950's when I was between 5 and 10 years old. It seems just like yesterday. As with many families during that time, missing church service was not an option. Even though we had to walk down a dusty road and cross over a creek to get there, we were always on time for Sunday school. In fact, we walked three and a half miles one way. I was always afraid to cross over the wooden foot-bridge to get across the creek because I would look down and see the water between the boards. When I would say, "I'm scared!" Momma would reply, "Girl, you better get across that bridge!" I would go back a distance from the bridge and then run with all my might so I could cross over in a hurry without seeing the water underneath. I learned to compensate for my fears by being strong.

When we would arrive at church, I always helped Daddy gather wood for the old potbelly stove that stood in the middle of the room in the front of the church by the pulpit. It was our only source of heat and someone had to get there early and get the fire going. My stepfather was what they called a steward, and he was responsible for making sure everything was ready for Sunday school and church services. Daddy, my mother, a few other people and we children would gather around the heater and warm our hands while we waited for church to start. We were always the first to arrive and the last to leave.

Back then, we had Sunday school every week, but church was on the first and third Sundays of the month. On the Sundays when the preacher came to have church, there would be a bigger crowd and I could see some of my cousins from school. We would sit there smiling back and forth at each other. We didn't dare talk or act out because back then, parents would give you a good backhand slap across the mouth. My mother was an usher and she didn't tolerate any foolishness. Sometimes, I felt a little restless, but when the church service started, I was moved by the slow, grinding sound of the meter hymns. These songs always stirred something on the inside of me. One of the deacons or one of the women would lead the group by calling out, "I came to Jesus as I was, weary, worn and sad. I found in him a resting place and he has made me glad." The rest of the church would join in and sing the words slowly and sadly. Some of the women would cry and rock back and forth, or raise their hands praising God. I didn't understand it, and it was a little scary. But, something about it made me know that God was real and he helped people who were sad.

Sunday school was happier than church. We sang songs like, *Yes, Jesus Loves Me.* The only time I really felt special was when we sang that song. I never told anyone how I felt, and that was probably because I couldn't explain it. In my heart, I knew that if no one else loved me, Jesus did. I believed the words to the song and I loved Jesus in my own childlike way. I wanted to know more about Him, so I paid close attention in Sunday school. At the time, I didn't know that these early childhood experiences were creating a love for God that would eventually develop into a deeper, stronger relationship with Him.

During my childhood, I always felt like my mother liked my sister Berdie and my brother David better than me. We were all two years apart in age. I was the oldest; Berdie was next, and David was the youngest. No matter what I did, I couldn't please my mother. She would fuss at me and beat me for the least little thing I did wrong. Sometimes, she beat me so hard that I would just cry out to God for help. Something inside of me said, "Be strong!" So, I tried not to cry. I felt like she was beating me because she resented me for some reason. She had had me out of wedlock and my birth father had rejected her. It seemed like I reminded her of him so, out of anger toward him, she would beat me.

Momma always made a difference in how she treated me compared to how she treated Berdie and David. I believed it was because they were born when she was married to my stepfather and I represented the shame of an unwanted pregnancy. I loved my stepfather and called him Daddy because he married Momma when I was less than two years old. He was the only father that I knew. He treated me with kindness and never whipped me. He always said, "Mamie, you're a good girl." But, he didn't dare go against Momma when she was beating me.

Momma whipped Berdie sometimes, but never like she beat me. Berdie would feel sorry for me and say, "Mamie, the reason Momma keeps beating you is because you won't cry! You should do like me and start crying *before* she hits you." It seemed I just couldn't be like Berdie. I didn't think I deserved a beating in the first place, so I refused to cry. All the beatings I got made me feel that Momma hated me. There were days when I wondered why I had ever been born. In my innocent way, I wondered if anyone *really* wanted me. I just wanted to disappear. During these moments of despair and insecurity, I would go into my shell like a turtle and spend time dreaming of faraway places and happiness. I dreamed that a handsome man would find me, marry me, and take me away. We would live in a nice house and be happy together. I thought that would be my only escape.

At the age of eight, I started hearing rumors that my stepfather was not my *real* father. While listening to comments, my ears perked up and I wanted to know more. I thought, *"Even if my stepfather was not my real father, he had always been there for me."* In fact, I found out later that my mother was engaged to my stepfather before he left to serve in the United States Marines. While he was away, she became pregnant. However, when my stepfather returned, he still married my mother and helped her take care of me. My stepfather treated me as his own child and never hurt me in anyway.

When I think about Momma and Daddy, I must say that opposites *do* attract. Momma was an entrepreneur from her heart. She was a very resourceful person and could always *make* things happen. These characteristics, coupled with faith, made her an extraordinary woman. It seemed there was nothing in the world my mother couldn't do. She intimidated men because of her ability to accomplish much. Dad was more reserved, laid back and quiet. Mom was the one that knew how to get the job done no matter what it took! Seeing the strength in my mother encouraged me, and I wanted to be like her. She was my role model in that she had great faith and determination. She set high standards for everyone, and I could never quite measure up. Imperfection made her angry. I hated to make her angry, but I always seemed to have a way of doing just that.

At the tender age of 12, I became curious as to who my *real* father was. Putting together all of the bits and pieces of information overheard from conversations, I started my search. I understood that my birth father had an affair with my mother, left Georgia the year I was conceived, and moved to Trenton, New Jersey, not knowing that my mother was pregnant. I was an inquisitive child and could always figure out a way to get things done. After all, I was my mother's daughter and because I had so much responsibility, I didn't think like a typical 12 year old. I did what other 12-year-old children may not have done, I wrote to the police department in Trenton, New Jersey and asked if they knew of a man with the name that everyone said that of my father. To my surprise, I was furnished with the information along with his home address. Of course, my parents didn't know this. When I received the response, I became frightened because now it seemed there may be some validity to rumors and I wondered what my mother would do if she knew.

One day shortly after that, my mother's female friend from New Jersey, who came to Georgia from time to time, visited us . I wondered if she knew my father. Her visit heightened my interest in my identity, and I began sorting through all the bits and pieces of information, forming my own conclusions, except that I was not able to share with anyone my newly found secret. One year, my mother's friend, who I later found out was my biological father's sister, brought me a box of nice clothing for Christmas. She also brought gifts for my siblings, but I got more than everyone else did. I enjoyed the special attention, but I wondered, *Why is this woman so nice to me? Why does she show me such love and concern?* I wanted to believe it was because I was the oldest, but by then all doubt was gone. I knew there was definitely something to the stories I had heard.

In the meantime, I wrote a letter to the man at the address that the police had provided. Astonishingly, there was a response. Being a child, I had not thought through what I would say or do if he responded, I just wanted to know if he was my real father. I had no idea he was happily married with three children. My letter caused serious problems for him and his family. I felt so guilty for what I had done. Of course, my mother was told about what I did. Now that the truth had come out, I was in *big* trouble with my mother. I had never seen Momma this angry before. Again, she beat me. This time I knew she would *kill* me. From that point on, her verbal and physical abuse got worse. When she beat me, I would wish that my stepfather would speak up and help me. He remained silent most of the time. He would say to me privately, "Your mother is wrong for treating you like that," but Daddy would seldom disagree with what Momma said or did. After all, *she* was the mover and shaker in the family.

During the formative years, I became more and more interested in Sunday school. My teacher began praising me for how well I could read. He let me read the lesson aloud for the adult class. I was so pleased. I felt special—a child reading to her elders. The very thought of being asked to participate in the adult class encouraged me to read more and be prepared to share in the lessons. I never wanted to disappoint them. I will never forget the lesson I heard one Easter Sunday when I was ten years old. The Sunday school lesson was about how Peter denied Jesus. This really struck my heart that he was Jesus' friend and he denied him. I said to myself, and have held to it until this day, "I will *never* deny Jesus!" Time moved on, and by the time I was 12 or 13 years old, I was teaching the adult Sunday school class all by myself.

Teaching the adult Sunday school class was just one of the things in my life that pushed me into the adult world. Consequently, my life as a child was short lived. Since I was the oldest child, I grew up quickly because I was expected to take on adult responsibilities early in my life. My maternal grandmother lived with us until she died when I was eight years old. She was very intelligent and had great wisdom. My mother didn't like housework, so she was out doing good deeds for the neighbors and church people and left me and the other children at home with my grandmother. Big Momma Rose, as we called her, took me under her guidance and taught me how to cook and clean. After she died, I took on the household tasks like washing, cleaning and preparing meals for the family.

Having so much adult responsibility made me frown at childish things. My siblings and cousins seemed much too silly for me. They liked to play with dolls and toys and would spend hours playing hide and seek. Those things never appealed to me. My sister Berdie really enjoyed being a child. While she played with her doll, I was busy learning adult things. From my earliest memories, I wanted to wear high heel shoes and fancy hats. To this day, I still like wearing high heels and hats.

After my mother saw how good I was at housework, she practically turned the household over to me. When the family began to depend almost solely on me to cook and clean, I began telling them how things should be done and what they should do. I could see things that needed improving and had ideas of how we could go about making them happen. However, like many parents of that time, my parents always reminded me that children were to be seen and not heard. In many ways, I had the responsibility of an adult, but was not allowed the freedom to speak my opinion like one. I was caught between being an adult and being a child. I felt like a misfit. As a result, I wanted to grow up quickly so I could fit in.

Berdie, David and I grew up in the countryside in poverty. It was difficult for my parents to support the family because of their limited skills and substandard high school education, so they resorted to sharecropping as a way of life. Sharecropping was hard work with very little financial pay off. I remember them purchasing food on credit since they had to wait for the crops to come in before they had any money. Sadly, most of the time, by the end of the harvest season they still didn't have any money. I would get angry because we sometimes had to stay out of school to work on the farm. Eventually, it became commonplace that we would spend our holidays working for someone else. Seeing my parents struggle year after year with very little return motivated me to strive for more in my life.

As a sharecropper's daughter, my mother would say, "Mamie, you can either go chop cotton, pick beans, peas or peaches or stay home and baby-sit." I didn't want to stay home and baby-sit, so I chose to go into the fields and work. We worked from sun up to sun down. Being in the fields with the older people, I overheard their conversations and felt like I understood adults better than I understood children. The work was hard, but I could keep up with the best of them.

The adults were amazed at how much work I could do. They often said, "That girl is so *smart*! She's going to make something out of herself!" They saw my potential, and that made me feel special. I learned so much from being around them that my heart was drawn totally away from children my own age. By the age of twelve, I thought and acted like an adult.

I began to organize our house and change furniture around and did everything I could to try to make our home-life better. I tried to make everyone feel good by planning little birthday surprises. One day, I discovered the Sears & Roebuck catalogue. It opened up a completely new world to me. When we got a catalogue, I would flip through the pages in awe of all the beautiful and shiny new things it had to offer. I'd look through it over and over again and dream of having the best appliances and wearing cute shoes and the latest fashions. I knew from those beautiful, bright pages that there were much better things in this world than what we had. All of a sudden, my dreams and aspirations began to extend beyond the cotton fields of Griffin, Georgia. I wanted more! I was no longer content with where I was. I *knew* there was a better life and I wanted it. I dreamed of moving far away from Griffin.

It was around this time that my biological father requested to meet me, and my parents agreed to let me go back to New Jersey with his sister the next time she came to visit my mother in Georgia. You can't imagine what it was like to leave my little country community and ride the train to Trenton, New Jersey. It felt like my dreams were coming true. I was beginning my journey to freedom.

I didn't know what would come of this trip, but it *had* to

be good. After living in the South, having to work hard in the fields, being poor and seemingly hated by my mother, I thought New Jersey would be a place of happiness for me. After all, my birth Dad had asked to meet me. Maybe this trip would be my means of escape.

Shortly after arriving in New Jersey, I met some of my siblings and cousins and their friends. I was awkwardly introduced to my sister and two brothers and their mother. While there, most of the time I lived with my aunt. This was a very traumatic experience for me being around all strangers. Of course, the neighbors obviously had heard of the situation, and came by to check me out to make their own determination of whether I looked like my supposed birth father or not. He was a very fair-skinned man in complexion and I was dark-skinned. It was apparent that they wondered whether I was really his child since I looked nothing like him. I was the exact image of my mother.

My female cousin introduced me to her friends, and my aunt took us on an outing to Coney Island. I was never so excited in my entire life. I got to see the Statue of Liberty, rode on carnival rides, and ate cotton candy. It was all wonderful! I could not believe I was having so much fun. I had never been free to do these childlike things before! It was like being in heaven!

My father had an expensive motorcycle. He belonged to a motorcycle club and he would take me for rides on his big, shiny motorcycle. It was as if he was showing off for me. I thought, *"This is great!"*

One day, my cousin, who was about my age, and her friends

were going to the city swimming pool and asked me to join them. Reluctantly, I went, even though I had no desire to get into the water. I was a little afraid of the water because once our school class went on a field trip to a swimming pool and someone pushed me into the pool. I nearly drowned. So, instead of getting in the water while at the pool, I played around with some of her friends. When I went to use the restroom, one of her male friends came in behind me and raped me. I was so afraid that I was paralyzed. I had never had any sexual interactions before and I couldn't believe what was happening. What could I do? I was devastated and humiliated. I had to pull myself together and walk out of the bathroom. Apparently, everyone else thought it was a joke! When I came out, they laughed and teased me. Even today, the pain and humiliation of that moment is just as fresh as if it happened yesterday.

I went back to my aunt's house, but was afraid to tell her what had happened. I hated facing my cousins and her friends, feeling ashamed of what had happened, and knowing that they saw me as the inexperienced country bumpkin. I asked myself, "How can I ask to leave early from the trip I so desperately wanted." I reasoned that I had to stay until the end of my planned summer vacation. Everyday I felt humiliated, degraded, and angry. I wanted to get revenge for what had happened to me. I could not understand why my cousin would not tell her mother. How could she expect me to want to go anywhere with her? In my resentment, I isolated myself and cried. That was my way of being protected from them until it was time to return home. I began crying almost every day. My aunt thought I was just homesick. She and my father did everything they could to make things better for me, but neither of them had any idea what had happened.

When the time came, I returned home with a broken heart and a secret. I would never tell anyone what happened to me for fear that my mother would beat me even the more and blame *me* for what happened. I found myself weeping a lot, staying alone, and starring into space. My best friend at school kept asking me, "Mamie, why are you crying and acting so different? Is something wrong?" I denied that anything was wrong.

Prior to going to New Jersey, my school experience was mostly all positive because it was one of the few places where I felt appreciated. I made very good grades and I had favor with the teachers. My teachers took a special interest in me and began to say, "She's smart." Those words ignited something in me like pouring gasoline on warm coals. I tried harder and harder to be the smartest student in the class. I thought if I could please my teachers, maybe they would help me; and they did. Reading constantly at school, home, and church gave me a great command of the English language and the self-assurance to stand before people and do recitations. Because I read so well, the teachers often selected me for leading roles in plays, recitals and special events. Eventually, I represented our school in the district and state oratorical contests. At times, I didn't have the proper clothes to participate in these activities, but there was always a teacher who gave me what was needed.

There were three teachers in particular who were very kind to me and helped me through these tough times: Mrs. Margaret Kendall, Mrs. Josephine Johnson and Mrs. Patricia

Head. They embraced and encouraged me and reached out to my parents to let them know they saw something special in me. They wanted to help. Mrs. Patricia Head didn't have children, so she would sometimes ask me to visit her on the weekend and spend the night. All of them invested in my life and wanted me to succeed. Occasionally spending the night with them, I was exposed to what it was like to live in a nice home and have nice things. I made up my mind, "This is what I also want for my family."

Being cared for by these teachers made me think, *"This is what it must have been like for Esther when she was preparing to go before the king."* I believed I was being prepared for something big! God was clearly ordering my steps. Although I didn't know it then, the experiences I had and the skills I learned as a child would help me survive later in life. God was developing strength of character in me that would sustain me during difficult times. God was moving behind the scenes to get me where He wanted me to be.

After my experiences in New Jersey, my behavior began to change at school. I was always bitter and angry, and I wanted to fight. When boys said anything to me, I wanted to clobber them with my fist. By now, I was 13 years old and was voted our 8th grade Homecoming Queen. My escort acted a little fresh towards me, so I punched him out. Nobody was going to disrespect me again. Later, another male classmate wrote me a letter saying how much he liked me. I confronted him and punched him out. After those incidents, I became labeled as a bully. The girls began to call me names, so I lit in on them, also. My teachers, who had previously been so impressed with me, could not understand why my behavior had changed. Suddenly, I began doing things that caused me to have to go to the principal's office. My mother began to beat me more and more for my behavior at school. The more she beat me, the tougher I became. I refused to shed another tear. That decision caused her to inflict more pain upon me.

In either the 8th or the 9th grade, I can't quite remember which, I was tested and scored 117 or 119 on the standard I.Q. test. My teachers were even more impressed. They saw my intellectual potential and encouraged me to continue to study and keep my grades up. Well it seemed like the more I was encouraged by my teachers and earned good grades, the more I was hated by my fellow students. The teachers encouraged me, but the students referred to me as the "Teacher's Pet." I resented that because nobody wanted to be my friend. I felt alone.

By then, I was a young, angry teenager and bitterness had become roasted in me. One of my teachers encouraged me to run track, which I did. I enjoyed playing sports, particularly softball and basketball. Playing sports became an outlet for me and I developed a sense of belonging with the team until one day at basketball practice, the coach yelled and cursed at me. I walked off the court to never return. I would not tolerate disrespect! The pain of rejection had reared its ugly head again, causing me to react in negative ways. This time I decided to stay away from everybody to protect my feelings.

In spite of being angry a lot, I was a hard worker. In fact, working was a way of digging me out of the hole I seemed to be in. My work ethic at home and school began to pay off financially. When the word spread that I could be counted on to get things done, many of the neighbors wanted me to work for them. I started working for different white people, and I did whatever they wanted done. Sometimes I would help serve guests at a house party. Once I even helped in a floral shop. Another time, I took care of someone's elderly mother, helping her get her food and get ready for bed. Sometimes I would be asked to water people's plants when they were on vacation, or I would wash and iron their clothes and clean the house. I occasionally cared for someone's children. My schedule became so hectic that I would work at home and then work odd jobs after school and on Saturdays.

Being paid for my work was a blessing because it gave me the opportunity to make some money, which helped make things better for all of us. My parents seemed to have been content to live without electricity and other modern conveniences, but I wanted more. So I began saving a few dollars from my pay and eventually paid for the family to get electricity for the first time. That first day I went to the switch and turned on the lights was so exciting. What a miracle! No more lighting kerosene lamps and holding them up so I could see how to read late at night after the family had gone to bed. No more getting ready for school by lamp light early in the morning before the sun came up. We were making progress. In the back of my mind was a dream that one day I would do something great. Deep in my heart, I knew that at some point I would leave this lifestyle and move on to something bigger and better.

I will never forget an August day in 1960. It was during our annual revival when a female evangelist began to pray for people who attended the service. She was speaking in tongues, something I had never heard before. She laid her hands on my forehead, and the next thing I remember I was getting up off the floor. Something happened on the inside of me that changed my life forever. None of us knew about the power of the Holy Spirit and the anointing, but I began to hear people say, "Mamie has not been the same since that woman preacher did something to her."

After that night, the Lord began to speak and reveal things to me. When I would share these revelations with others, they began calling me a fortune-teller. I really became afraid because that made me feel uncomfortable. I had always been told that fortune-tellers were evil and wicked, and I didn't want to be a part of *anything* evil. I decided to stop sharing my dreams and visions, but they kept coming. The Lord began to reveal things about people around me. He showed me things that were sometimes positive and sometimes negative. I had to keep them in my heart and not share them with anyone because they probably wouldn't understand. I began to pray more, and every opportunity I had I would pray publicly. In fact, it was a tradition that a deacon or officer would place a chair out front for someone to kneel and pray. Interestingly enough, I thought that chair was for me. I felt like I could get a prayer through to God. My confidence and faith that God would hear me made a place for me in the church. I was often asked to pray not only in my own church, but in other churches as well. I didn't know it then, but the hand of God was granting me *favor* in the midst of what I thought was a sad, poverty-stricken childhood.

By the early sixties, our family had moved into a better

house, and my parents were no longer sharecroppers. My mother worked at the school. She would serve food in the cafeteria during the day, and after school, she would clean up the school building. I was expected to help her clean after school. My daddy worked at a boat factory. Even though my parents had better jobs, they still bought groceries on credit. For some odd reason, that really bothered me. I thought, "Will this cycle ever end?" I just said, "God, please help me so I will never have to charge groceries or gas." To this day, I have never owned a gas charge card. At an early age, it was etched in my mind that it was not the best thing to be indebted to others. This idea was affirmed in my life when I read the Scripture in Proverbs 22:7 that states, "The rich rule over the poor and the borrower is servant to the lender."

During this time, I was still doing really well in school, and my behavior was mostly controlled since I stayed by myself a lot. It almost seemed like I was earning my mother's respect. She was very proud of the fact that I was an honor roll student. For many years, it had seemed that I could never please my mother. Even when I was washing and cleaning at home, it was never good enough. I remember days when I had scrubbed clothes on the rub board, rinsed them and hung them on the clothesline, only to have my mother come home, look at them and say, "Get those dirty clothes off the line! How could you hang those dirty clothes on that clothesline? Redo them!" I was distressed and would hurriedly take them down and start again, frantically trying to please her. With the passage of time, my mother seemed to be growing less agitated with me. She supported me in school, came to Parent Teacher Association meetings and did whatever she could to support my education. She was especially proud of my academic achievements.

In the middle of my teenage years, my high school classes became less interesting and challenging for me. I was easily bored and wanted to skip over some things and move on. In some ways, I was impatient and wanted to get on with life. I had had adult responsibilities for a long time, and before long, my distractions led me to make some wrong choices. Because of the teasing I often received, I had isolated myself from most students in school. Eventually, loneliness overcame me and my need for love and attention came to the forefront of my life. I began to look for love in the wrong place. I entertained conversations with a fellow male student who was one grade ahead of me. We became what I thought was friends. When he smiled at me and began showing me special attention, I felt loved and cared for in a way I had never felt before. The attention of a man was what I had dreamed about. I wanted love. I wanted to be treated with tenderness, so it was easy to give in to his sexual advances. Eventually, the relationship I thought was love lost its tenderness, and he was raping me repeatedly, saying he loved me and wanted to marry me. Since I had never had anyone actually tell me they loved me, I fell for his deception hook, line and sinker. Not knowing that he wanted only sex, I felt important. As a result, I made myself available to satisfy his sexual needs. In other words, he owned my body. There were times when he wanted to be with me that I found a way to be with him at any cost. After all, my emotional needs were being met while he gained sexual favors.

Around December of 1961, I realized I was pregnant.

I didn't know what to do. It seemed like my whole world had fallen apart. I knew my mother would beat me. Secretly, I cried because I was so afraid of what people would say, especially after I had been so faithful in church, prayed so fervently and was a Sunday school teacher. I thought to myself, *"What would my teachers say who had put time and money into helping me achieve?"* I was ashamed and embarrassed. Who could I turn to? I couldn't tell *anyone*, so I tried to hide my pregnancy as much as possible. Since it was winter when I found out, I wore my coat as often and as long as I could. When the weather changed, I made sure my clothes were loose so my pregnancy would not show.

In about the fifth month of my pregnancy, my mother became suspicious of my behavior. She asked, "Girl, why are you laying around here sleeping and tired all the time? You pregnant? " She badgered me until, finally, shaking fearfully, I confessed, "Yes, ma'am, I'm pregnant." That Thursday night was one I will never forget. Momma became hysterical. In fact, she lost control and beat me until blood was streaming from my nose. She beat me unmercifully! My back was bleeding from switch marks left on it. My siblings were crying for her to stop and eventually Daddy spoke up and said, "You ought to be ashamed of yourself for beating her like that!" She said to me, "Get out of my house before I kill you!" Frightened, hurting and crying, I left the house wondering where I was going. I started to walk along the country road, and a family friend who happened to be driving by picked me up and took me to my aunt's house. I stayed at my aunt's house a couple of days. She asked Momma about what happened. Of course, Momma didn't recall all that she had done because she had been drinking. Whenever she took a drink of alcohol, she was always meaner and tougher. She seemed remorseful, but she never acknowledged it.

My emotional pain was deep. I was so hurt. I had never felt loved by my mother and now when I needed her most she threw me out – she had abandoned me. I just wanted *someone* to love me. I cried out, "God please help me!" I didn't know where I would go. My aunt had taken me in temporarily. I was pregnant and homeless. That night I cried and prayed. I thought of suicide, but I kept hearing the song we sang in Sunday school, "Yes, Jesus loves me. Yes, Jesus loves me. Yes, Jesus loves me, for the Bible tells me so." Soon, I made contact with my boyfriend and told him what had happened. He spoke with his aunt and she agreed that I could come and live with them until he finished school in a few weeks.

That Monday, I returned to school as usual since the school officials didn't know I was pregnant. I wanted to finish my 11th grade year, but girls were not allowed to go to school pregnant in those days. My mother, who was still working at the school, went in and informed the principal that I was pregnant. He called me into his office and I was asked to withdraw from school or *prove* that I was not pregnant. The one thing I had to hold on to was now being taken from me. I had to withdraw from school just a few weeks before finishing 11th grade. It seemed like my life was over.

Up to this point, my mother had bragged to others about my good grades and what a smart child I was, even though at home she verbally, physically, and emotionally abused me. I felt more like a possession, more like a workhorse, than a person.

Now that I was pregnant, my mother seemed to hate me even more. I was part of a generation of women who had gotten pregnant by someone who didn't marry them. Big Momma Rose had had Momma before she was married; Momma had had me before she was married, and now *I* was having a baby out of wedlock. I needed a chance to start over. With no real home, I again cried out to God, "Lord, please send me a husband that will provide for me and my baby!" Within a few months, the Lord answered my prayers. I met the man of my dreams when I was seven months pregnant. It was as if I was God's little acorn. He had helped me push through my shell and soon I would grow into a sapling. My branches didn't look too good, but my roots were deep in God's soil and He would help me become a tall, sturdy oak tree. This pregnancy seemed like a terrible detour away from what I had dreamed of for my life, but my life would take many twists and turns as God moved me closer to my dream of starting over and to my destiny.

A NEW BEGINNING

It was the Friday before Easter in April 1962. I was living with my boyfriend Ralph's aunt, Mrs. "Chunk", who happened to be a neighbor to Joseph Harris. One day Joseph stopped by to visit them. I came into the room while he was there and was introduced to him. I was a little reluctant to enter the room because I was seven months pregnant and had no husband. I already felt ashamed, so I was uneasy about anyone who might judge me. After a very brief introduction, I excused myself and went back to my chores. I was always busy, just like Martha, the sister of Mary in the Bible. Work was a way of life for me, and I was used to it. At the time, it helped to keep my mind off my situation.

A few days later, Joseph stopped by the house again to visit with the family. This time he engaged in a conversation with me. I shied away from talking to him too much as I didn't want him to ask me anything about my situation. Withdrawing from him was my way of rejecting him and protecting myself. During our conversation, I learned that his twin sister taught at the same school where my mother worked and that several of his relatives were my classmates. I also found out that his grandfather was the founder and pastor of the community church, and that he lived with them and was a father figure to him. He openly shared facts about his family and life with me. Joseph told me that his mother was the only daughter his grandfather had, but that he had a lot of sons.

While living in he community with his family, I got to see and meet all of them. They were raised in a Christian home and were devoted to the Lord. Joseph's father was tall and thin, and his mother was short and petite. Even though his mother was small in stature, only about 5'1" tall, she was powerful; the epitome of a Proverbs 31 woman. I found it hard to believe that this little woman had given birth to two sets of twins and four other children. Feeling some reluctance to giving birth myself, I thought, "Eight children! She's must be a pro at having babies." I was fearful of giving birth, mostly because I had heard a few women talk of their experiences. Up to this point in my life, I had been very strong and able to get through almost anything, but now I wondered if delivering a baby would be more than I could handle.

Joseph continued to come by and visit, and eventually we shared information about ourselves and began to trust each other a little more each day. We shared our painful experiences and our desire to overcome the many challenges we were facing. In time, we became friends, but I purposely kept my friendship with Joseph at a distance. In my heart, I hoped to marry my boyfriend Ralph. He had promised that we would get married in June after his high school graduation and before the baby was to be born in July. Little did I know that this was an empty promise.

I continued to live with Aunt Chunk, taking care of her three grandchildren and maintaining the house in exchange for my livelihood. Eventually, Ralph didn't come around as often as before. Once when he came, he asked me to help him prepare a term paper in one of his classes so that he could graduate. I completed the assignment for him and he graduated with his class.

After Ralph's graduation, he had a change of heart about our relationship and no longer wanted to get married. He decided to join the Army and see the world, without me and the baby. My worst nightmare had become a reality. I thought, *"What am I going to do?"* After all, I was living with Ralph's aunt and cousins. My heart was broken and I wanted to die. I was afraid of what would happen to my child and me. Feeling abandoned and hopeless, I went to the pharmacy and purchased some arsenic to commit suicide. When I left the drugstore, I kept hearing that song from Sunday school in my heart, *"Yes Jesus loves me, for the Bible tells me so."* The words repeatedly played in my ears until I threw the arsenic in the trash and went home.

When Aunt Chunk and the rest of his family heard of Ralph's decision, they tried to intervene by coaching the relationship in hopes he would change his mind. By this time, I was wobbling. I was eight months pregnant and already feeling miserable. After hearing Ralph's decision, I spiraled into a state of depression, thinking how alone I was. I felt that no one cared about my baby and me not even the child's father. I didn't know whom to turn to. I was a frightened 16-year-old living away from her parents and family, not to mention I was pregnant, had no job and no education. Grief soon overtook every inch of my heart.

Joseph was in the Navy at the time and was stationed in Marietta, GA. Most of the time, he would commute to and from Griffin. Whenever he would come home, he would make sure he was in contact with me. I began to like him a little more each time we talked. I was really attracted to his sharp Navy uniform. He looked so handsome. Sometime later, he shared with me that he was recovering from a long-term relationship that had recently ended. He had a seven-year-old son from that relationship. When he told me this, I thought, *"Did he abandon the son's mother the way Ralph had abandoned me?"* If so, I wanted to have nothing to do with him.

Joseph assured me that it was his desire to marry the mother of his child. In fact, she didn't want to marry him. I initially found this hard to believe, but later I found out from her it was true. During the few months I had known Joseph, he showed me kindness and encouraged me to hang in there with my pregnancy. I was beginning to see his true character.

On July 7, I went into labor. I had no idea what labor pains would be like until they started. I had a high tolerance for pain, but this was unreal! I lay in bed at Aunt Chunk's house in the sweltering summer heat. It was scorchingly hot and sticky, and neither she nor anybody else I knew had air conditioning. I was sweating and suffering. In between contractions, I thought, *"If only I could be in an air-conditioned hospital room, maybe having this baby wouldn't be so difficult."* The reality was that no one I knew went to the hospital to have a baby because they didn't have any money, and they surely didn't have a job that provided health benefits. Almost everyone I grew up around struggled just to feed and clothe their families. They had their babies at home with the assistance of a mid wife. I had to do the same.

When a labor pain would hit me, I'd cry out to God to have mercy! Aunt Chunk contacted my mother and she came to be by my side. She helped coach me through my difficult delivery. Even though she had forced me to leave home, we began to restore our relationship. My son, Greg, was born at home through natural childbirth. He was a healthy, hungry baby who ate constantly. I had mixed emotions about the whole ordeal. Suddenly, I was a 16-year-old mother with another human being depending on me. I couldn't imagine any man wanting a woman with a child that he had not fathered. I began to wonder, *"What will become of us?"* I didn't know where the resources would come from to support us. Once the baby was born, Ralph came by a couple of times, but I knew I had to wade through this tragedy without him.

Joseph was on duty when the baby was born. After he came home from work that day, someone told him that the baby had been born. To my surprise, he showed up with a gift for the baby – six cans of Pet Milk! That's what everyone fed their babies back then; there was no special formula. My heart was touched by his sensitivity and compassion.

After Greg was born, I prayed and cried that the Lord would make a way for me to survive. We went to live with my high school friend, Bertha, and her mother. Bert had always kept in touch with me and was there for me even after I dropped out of school. She and I bonded even more during the difficult period of my pregnancy. Joseph didn't like the idea of me moving and not having a home of my own. I was afraid to let him in on my decision beforehand because, secretly, I kept hoping that Ralph would change his mind and rescue me. Finally, it dawned on me that Joseph was the man God had sent as an answer to my prayers.

At first, it was difficult for us to trust each other. We each thought the other might return to the previous relationship. Finally, we both realized that God had a hand in *our* relationship. I began to see Christ through Joseph's actions. He was a good man. He began to say, "I'm going to marry you one day." I thought to myself, "He's just kidding me." After all, Joseph was a very handsome man. He had a lot of women to choose from, so why would he choose me? After all, I had a child, no education and nothing to offer him except myself.

It seemed as though these things did not matter to Joe. Eventually, he became my greatest encourager. He had confidence in me and we became the best of friends. We bonded because of our mutual need for healing from our pasts. Both of our children's parents had moved on with their lives. We were two broken people dealing with rejection, yet wanting to re-establish trust and start a relationship with someone who genuinely loved us for who we were.

Nearly a year later in August of 1963, I had a revelation confirming that Joseph was to become my husband and that he would preach the Word of God. At first, I thought it was just my own impulse, but I realized later that it had indeed come from God. When I shared with him that he would preach, he was a little upset and asked me not to say it. Just his reaction let me know that this was not the first time he had heard this. He seemed as if he was resisting the idea of his preaching, but I could not refrain from speaking words I knew had come from God. Even though he grew up in a godly home, was raised by godly parents and his grandfather was the pastor of the local church, he didn't want to hear that *he* would be a preacher. Joseph had seen the not so great side of ministry and he knew the hurts and pains a pastor often encountered.

When we both realized that our lives would be united, we worked through our differences and became more acquainted with each other's families. Our relationship grew, and two years after meeting we were married in our family church immediately following the Sunday morning worship service. In fact, we already had our license, but were not sure what day we would get married. We had not worked out the details. We knew we couldn't afford a wedding, so we just decided to marry quickly. Neither Joe's nor my parents knew. To our surprise, we were the first couple that my pastor ever married. He was just as nervous as we were. We didn't have a ring, so the pastor loaned Joe his wedding band to place on my finger. We were married on April 4, 1964, almost two years to the day that we first met. We got an apartment and three rooms of inexpensive furniture on sale. We were thrilled because we finally had a home of our own!

When we married, Joe was still in the Navy, assigned to Marietta. During this time, his military career was challenged and he was almost kicked out. He had a rigorous schedule and no reliable means of transportation. He was sometimes late for work. Given the strictness of military customs, it was the grace of God that kept him in the Navy. Nevertheless, he was reduced in rank and went from working as a personnel clerk to being a dishwasher on kitchen detail. His career was transformed from a dream to a nightmare, which made our marriage shaky. Joe turned to alcohol to reduce the strain, and that just made things worse. The alcohol robbed him of his self-esteem and he seemed to lose his motivation to advance in his career. Through prayer, he was able to start over and later retired from the Navy with an amazing 20-year career.

Once married, we were faced with deciding where we would attend church. Joe's family was highly recognized in the church community because of their involvement in his grandfather's church. They were all known for being great singers. I wanted to be a good wife to Joe, so I decided to follow him. His church had preaching on the second and fourth Sundays of the month, and my church had services on the first and third Sundays of the month. Actually, that meant I could attend both services, which I did for a while. But, it wasn't too long before I moved my membership to his church.

As a young couple, we began our life as husband and wife without knowing the many challenges that we would face. My life had been a tale of stress brought on by abuse, rejection and low self-esteem. In addition, I quickly found out that marriage brought even more stressful situations.

Sometimes life can be so difficult that it can cause one to give up and stop looking for light at the end of the tunnel. In my season of hopelessness, I just wanted to get out of the darkness that engulfed me. I couldn't see my way out of my situation, nor could I see how to move forward. I didn't want to live anymore; consequently, I tried to end my life. I tried to commit suicide. I know now that taking your own life is a selfish, cowardly way to get out of a situation instead of going through it, as God would have us do.

Shortly after Joe and I married, I got pregnant again. I gave birth to a premature, stillborn baby girl that weight one pound, six and a half ounces. I only got a glimpse of the baby and never held her. Due to hormonal imbalances after giving birth, my own pain and feelings of disappointment, I became consumed with grief. Just thinking about the stillborn child that I never had a chance to hold in my arms raised feelings of guilt and loss. Was God punishing me by not allowing me to have my husband's baby since I had had a child out of wedlock?

Without a clear understanding of what I was doing, I signed papers to permit the hospital to dispose of my baby without Joe seeing her. When I realized what I'd done, I was discouraged and disappointed. I longed for my baby girl. I wondered what it would have been like to hold her, feed her, and change her diapers. I was tortured by emotional grief from losing her. I desperately wanted another baby. I knew another baby would not replace the one I'd lost, but I wanted a child that represented the love that Joe and I had for each other.

A few months later, I was pregnant again. The day after I turned 19 years old, I gave birth to another baby girl, Sonya, who was born prematurely at two pounds and ten ounces. Having my husband's baby did not relieve my sense of guilt and shame. I experienced so much guilt that I sincerely believed that I was being punished by God. My doctor prescribed Valium to help calm my nerves. My body was worn out and I was emotionally drained. I had given birth to three babies within two years and I was a nervous wreck.

It was also during this time that I became the first African American to work at the previously segregated textile industry in our small hometown of Griffin. Moving into unfamiliar territory created more stress. At breaks and lunchtime, I often found myself sitting in the break room and cafeteria alone. Going to the bathroom and drinking water from the company fountains presented opportunities for the white employees to sneer and whisper about me.

Having white coworkers treat me this way made me wonder how fellow human beings could be so cruel. The sneering and whispering were just the beginning. Eventually, I saw more and more employees bring their personal thermos bottles to work and then quit drinking from the water fountain altogether. They often found excuses not to sit in the break room or in any chair where I had sat. The rejection was unbearable.

My life was out of control. I was overwhelmed by my job situation, caring for my two children, preparing for my GED test, and the responsibility of being a military wife whose husband was away on duty. On day, during my lunch hour at work, I took a handful of Valium in hopes escaping by ending my life. I wanted to find relief. After taking the Valium, I went across the street to a black-owned service station to seek solitude from my hostile work environment. I collapsed at the station. Someone called for an emergency vehicle and I was rushed to the hospital where my stomach was pumped. By the grace of God, my body was not damaged. My emotional state, however, required that I remain in the hospital Psychiatric Ward for several days. For some reason, God would not let me die. I knew then that I had to find out why God let me live.

After that experience, I had a hunger for life like never before. I made up my mind that I was going to live and raise my children. By then we had three children: Joe's son Larry, my son Greg, and our new baby girl, Sonya. Larry was very much a part of our lives. Unlike many situations where there is an angry stepmother involved, I developed a good relationship with Larry's mother. Amazingly, we became good friends and endured many hardships during the years while jointly raising Larry. Years later, I was able to lead Larry and his mother to a personal relationship with the Lord. Our friendship has spanned many years, indicative of a special bond that's not easily understood by others. She, Joe and I developed an unusual relationship.

After my suicide attempt, I had no family pastor to talk with, so I spent my time praying and talking with the Lord. I eventually came out of the depression, but wanted to get away from Griffin and all the painful things that had happened to me there.

I knew the Lord had answered my prayers when before two years of marriage Joe got military orders for duty at Grosse Isle, Michigan, near Detroit. At first, when I realized we were leaving Georgia, I was excited because it was another prayer being answered. I would be leaving my disappointments and memories behind.

An opportunity to start my life all over again. I felt like the Lord had rescued me. On the other hand, the thought of leaving everything I knew was more difficult than I thought. Joe left for Michigan a few months ahead of us to make sure we had living quarters when we arrived.

Joe left for Michigan a few months ahead of us to make sure we had living quarters when we arrived. Joe's brother, David, stayed with me and the two children to help us until Joe got things established for us in Michigan. In August of 1966, Joe returned to Griffin to take us to Michigan. By now, our families had bonded and with us leaving, they felt like part of their family was being taken away. Everyone expressed a lot of emotions, some positive and some negative. My parents felt like I was taking their grandchildren away from them. They asked, "Who will be your baby sitter for the children?" Coming from a very different mindset, I wondered, *"Where will I find work?"* We would be a 12-hour drive away from Griffin. It was 600 miles by car, and one and half hours by plane. We would be too far away for family members to help us, so we had to stand-alone. I did not realize at the time how difficult being away from family support would be with two small children and a husband in military service.

Leaving was very painful. Even though my parents wanted me and the children to stay in Griffin, I knew my place was with my husband. So, we packed up our small five-passenger car with the essentials and drove away from Griffin to make a new life in Michigan. Our furniture had already been packed by the Navy and would arrive at our new place in ten days.

When we arrived at Grosse Isle, Michigan, we were stunned.

There were no blacks, no one with whom we could identify. We could feel the tension, and we felt rejected before we even unpacked the car. We began to inquire of housing elsewhere. Instead of living on the Grosse Isle base, Joe made a sacrifice for his family and found housing at Selfridge Air Force Base where the people seemed welcoming and we felt safe. This meant that Joe would have a 65-mile commute one way.

I really hated seeing Joe travel so far in the early mornings on the freezing, snowy highways, going to and from work. This was unimportant to him because his primary concern was for the safety and happiness of his family. We had a four year old and a two year old. He wanted us to be in a safe, healthy environment where we would feel accepted.

Being away from everyone and everything familiar to us drew us closer together. All we had in this strange place was each other. Even still, with no family, no friends and no church home, we wondered if we had made the right decision.

When the furniture and personal items arrived, we moved in and our children began making new friends. One day, I was helping our son Greg get his bike out and he introduced me to his friend Geoff. Greg always made friends easily and was very popular because of his contagious smile. Later, I met Geoff's mother, Alma Lowry, and we started what became a lifelong friendship. Without the support of family, Alma was a blessing. She was there for me, lending support and a listening ear. Some time later, Alma's husband, who was in the Air Force was sent to Vietnam and she had to move back home to Pittsburgh. I really missed my friend. We stayed in touch and saw each other whenever possible.

During our time in Michigan, Joe decided to adopt Greg since we had no contact with his biological father. In fact, we had not heard from Ralph in several years and had no idea where he was. Consequently, we decided to file the paperwork for Greg's adoption. After filing the papers with the legal counsel, the adoption was granted in 1967. Joe fathered Greg as if he was his own biological child, loving and supporting him in every way.

While settling into our new life, I began looking for a job. As God would have it, I got a job after my very first interview. I began to get to know people around the base. My neighbor would baby-sit with the children for me until Joe got home in the evenings. I did shift work. I would see my children off to school and be home when they returned. Sometimes it required me to work a split shift to do this. I would work from 9 AM to 1 PM and then from 4 PM to 9 PM.

A short time later, I found out I was pregnant, and because of complications I had to quit my job. During the pregnancy, I was placed on bed rest for two months. The baby was born prematurely and weighed 3 pounds and 7 ounces. We named her Tina. She had to stay in the hospital for several weeks. Daily, I would go back and forth to the hospital to sit with her. This made for stressful times for our marriage and our family. Even though I was away from family and friends, God sent people I didn't know to help with the children. The people in the military community were very kind and supportive. They all seemed to chip in and help each other, knowing that they might also need help at some point. Our neighbors and friends were a tremendous blessing to us and our young children.

Since I was no longer working, Joe had to get a part-time job to make ends meet. We drew closer than ever, praying for our newborn, as well as Greg and Sonya. Tina, our newborn, was improving daily, and after almost three months, we finally brought her home. She quickly gained weight and developed into a fine, healthy baby. I was so thankful to God.

Juggling the house and three small children was a challenge. We decided to solicit the help of my sister, Berdie, to come live with us and help with the children. Having her there gave us support and a stronger sense of family. Joe and Berdie hit it off very well. By now, Joe was very popular on the base and was often called upon to sing at the club. Berdie would tag along sometimes. I mostly stayed home with the children. Occasionally, I would get a chance to hear and see him perform. By nature, Joe was a very quiet, reserved person, but when he got into his singing environment, he would liven up. He was energized by his passion for music.

While we were in Michigan, Poppa, Joe's grandfather, died. We couldn't all afford to travel with him to Griffin to the funeral. Because we lived so far away, we didn't get a chance to say goodbye to him, and this made us all very sad. The children had missed the opportunity to get to know their great-granddaddy.

After spending three and a half years in Michigan, it was time to move to a new duty station. When Joe received orders to report for duty on a ship, we knew he would have to leave his family for months at a time. I had to do something, but I was at a loss. I didn't know what to do. My first thought was to write our congressman. I didn't' know or care who I had to contact. I needed my husband to help me raise the three children. I had no idea that marrying this man in the sailor shirt, navy bell-bottoms, and sailor hat would mean that he would have to go on a Mediterranean ship and leave his family behind. In desperation, I wrote our congressman, explaining our situation and believing God for a miracle. One thing I knew how to do was pray, and I expected God to answer.

In a few weeks, we received an acknowledgement of my letter stating that they would consider my request, but that no promises could be made. Praise God! Two weeks later, Joe's orders were changed to sea duty in Rota, Spain with concurrent travel for his wife and children! Glory to God! We would have housing accommodations. My prayer was truly answered. In fact, I had to get out the atlas in order to see exactly where Rota, Spain was. I had never heard of it, but knew it must be a great place. It was a very exciting time for us, but sad for our family back in Georgia. We would be gone overseas at least three years, maybe longer.

Prior to leaving, we visited our families in Griffin for Christmas in December of 1969. When Joe's report date arrived, the rest of us had not yet received our passports. Because of this delay in receiving our passports, Joe left without us and arrived in Spain in January. Our household goods had left a few days before he left, so we moved into a hotel. Finally, in March, two months after Joe had left; we flew to Rota, Spain. We were so excited to see him and explore Spain.

We had no idea what Spain would be like. Several years before we had left hot, sunny Georgia with its red clay dirt, and gone to Michigan where the snow started in November and continued periodically until early spring. Now, we were in a world filled with bright, beautiful flowers, clear blue ocean waters and sandy beaches right outside our hotel window. We were amazed! It was certainly not Griffin.

Since our arrival was delayed, the housing that had been identified for us was no longer available. As a result, we ended up staying in a hotel for three more months, until June 1970 when we found housing on the local economy. Living in the hotel suite with three young children was very difficult. We had no stove or refrigerator. The noise and closeness of the quarters caused enormous strain in our marriage. I felt like Joe had an advantage, because at least he got to go to work everyday. I sat there day after day, week after week with nothing stimulating to do. I felt cooped up in this small space with just the noise and complaints of the children. I had to get out of the hotel room in order to maintain my sanity. I spent many days crying out to God, taking the children to the beach, walking and praying about my marriage and my purpose in life, and longing to be back home. Much of my thinking took place as I stared out at the endless vastness of the Atlantic Ocean.

We had many challenges. First, we had no telephone and no natural gas. We used a butane bottle for cooking and a kerosene heater for heating the rooms. Since we didn't speak Spanish, we had a language barrier. Getting everyday errands done was very difficult. Just trying to get people to understand what we needed was exhausting. This was *not* the Spain we had dreamed about, and I wanted to go back home. Somehow, Griffin, Georgia didn't seem that bad after all. Since we didn't live on base with the other Americans and had to live in a

Spanish community, we felt like outcasts once again. It seemed like I was always an outsider no matter where I went.

Finally, we settled in, got to know some people, and decided to make the best of the situation and our time together. Joe did everything he could to make us comfortable and to provide for us. He was assigned to a submarine squad and served on a tugboat with 12 other guys, which was considered choice duty. Even so, these were challenging times for our marriage and our children.

The pressure of the adjustments we had to make while learning to live in a foreign country and an unknown culture began to weigh heavily on us. I felt that if I could just find a job on the military base everything would be better. Unfortunately, jobs were hard to find and the same prejudices we experienced in the United States were also prevalent in Spain. Eventually, after several attempts, I got a job with the Navy Resale System, but it did not come easy. It was mandated by the Equal Employment Opportunity office. I was happy. I had a job and could get out of the house and meet people that I could relate to, American people.

From what we had heard, the overseas military community was like a close-knit family. The families tended to bond together and support each other. They interacted socially with each other. Generally, this was true, but segregation was still evident, so blacks had to find their own social outlets. We organized the VIP social club and the base commander allowed us full use of a vacant Quonset hut, which allowed us to make it our private club to hold parties and other social events. Joe was both one of the cooks and the singer for most events we held.

After six months of living in a Spanish community, we moved onto the military base where our home became the community house. Living on the main street gave everyone the idea they could just drop by any time, and the fact that we were very good hosts didn't help matters. People stopped by frequently. At times, it became very taxing, but we enjoyed it. I met many new people through work and invited many to our home. Sometimes I would cook, and other times everyone would bring a covered dish and we would fellowship together. Many military families were brought together because of the social gatherings we hosted. Although we developed new friends who became our family, this did not make up for the frustration we experienced when family members and loved ones passed away back in the States. It did not help that we were not able to go home for funerals, let alone go for a visit. Just the thought of being so far from home was a challenge. We were also distressed because our children didn't have their grandparents around. Spain was fun, but we yearned for home and family. I had prayed for a new beginning, but I wasn't sure this was exactly what I asked for. I found out that God answers prayers, but most often, He does it *His* way and not necessarily the way we expect.

GOD'S FAVOR

Proverbs 21:1 states, "The king's heart is a stream of water in the hand of the Lord, he turns it wherever he will." I cannot logically explain all the amazing things that have happened to me and for me through the years. I can only say that God's hand has always been on my life and His favor has gone before me to change the hearts of men to open doors for me and others. One thing I have learned is that the favor of God will take you places you never dreamed you could go. Not only will God bless you, but He will also bless those whose lives you touch and who touch your life. I know without a shadow of a doubt that your gift will make room for you and bring you before great men as Proverbs 18:16 states.

Jesus said, "Except you have the faith of a little child, you cannot enter into the Kingdom." I think of how God wants us to come to Him with a sincere and pure heart just like a child, with no reservations, no fear of failing, just total trust in Him, the all powerful, ever loving and unfailing God. This is the only way I can account for the miraculous blessings that God has poured out in my life.

When I think about my purpose in life, it's not hard to see that God uses me as a pioneer, which is one who goes before and paves the way for others. I often find myself breaking new ground that opens up opportunities for those around me. When a new path is being cleared in a wilderness, often there are obstacles like thickets and bushes and small trees that block the path; the terrain is usually rough with bumps and uneven ground; and there may be overhanging branches that obstruct the vision and the passageway. God needs pioneers like John the Baptist, who go before, clearing the path for all to see clearly as they move through the wilderness to meet our Lord and Savior Jesus Christ, the one who came to rescue the perishing. My purpose is to move out and pioneer paths. That's what I've always done and that's what I will continue to do.

My first pioneering experience takes me back to 1962, before Joe and I were married and when I began working in a textile factory in Locust Grove, Georgia. What a thrill it was to be there. I really needed a job and the building was air-conditioned. This was my opportunity to get out of the hot, humid summer weather in Griffin. Only those who have lived through the sultry summers in Georgia without air conditioning can appreciate the delight of working in an air-conditioned building. Hard work outside in the blistering Georgia sun would make anyone appreciate inside work. To add icing to the cake, this was a job, unlike chopping cotton, where I could *sit* and work. Truly, God was with me!

After working for a while in Locust Grove, the company prepared to integrate the textile factory in Griffin. I applied for the job and was hired. Now, I worked right at home and didn't have to commute. As God would have it, I was the first black American to integrate the textile industry at Griffin American Mills. This was quite an achievement for someone who had not finished high school and had a child born out of wedlock. Even though I was totally stressed by all things I had to endure at the factory, God used me to pave the way for other blacks to work in the textile industry.

I didn't get my high school diploma, but I did take the test and received my GED in December of 1964. Afterwards, when we left Georgia and moved to Michigan, I took the Civil Service test and became a test administrator. This began my Federal career that spanned 18 years. Also, while in Michigan, I became the first black to integrate the A&P food store in Mt Clemens. As I reflect on my accomplishments, I recognize that many of them came from the fact that I was never afraid to speak out about injustices. From early childhood, I learned to stand up for myself when I understood that no one else could plead my case as well as I could. I learned to pursue the things I wanted in life with a passion and a determination. I was never afraid of hard work; all I needed was a chance to prove myself. Coming to know Jesus and having an encounter with the Holy Spirit gave me a "holy boldness." I always knew that God was with me.

Looking back I realize how often God intervened. He intervened in Rota, Spain, and blessed my family and me. We had to live on the local economy because military base housing was unavailable when my children and I arrived after a three-month delay. Prior to coming, we had been told of the horrible problems with mildew in the houses made of plaster because of the heat and humidity in Spain. A few weeks before our arrival, two soldiers had tragically died. They had gone to sleep and left their kerosene heater on without proper ventilation. This news was unsettling.

Even though I had prayed for the family to accompany Joe, I knew that God would have to work a miracle for me to stay in Spain with the conditions we were hearing about. He did just that! We found out that the only homes in the area where we would live were made out of wood that did not mildew. Another factor that inhibited mildew was the fact that we lived very close to the coast. Additionally, our house had better ventilation than many houses, and we used space heaters during the winter months, which helped to dry things out. Again, God was faithful; He made a way for us in the desert.

It was also in Spain that God placed me in a position to open up opportunities for others. After we moved into our house and the family was settled, I began looking for a job. For several months, I applied for a variety of vacant positions without any response. I didn't know what to do. Shortly afterwards, I read in the *Stars and Stripes,* the military newspaper, that an investigation team with Colonel Frank Peters and Frank Render would be touring Europe to deal with issues affecting military personnel and their family members. I began to rejoice because I knew this was my opportunity to address the team with my own concerns and those of the community regarding employment. With passion and conviction, I pleaded my case, and the case of deserving military family members before the committee. Within ten days after our dialogue, I had a job working on the military base. This was a blessing from God.

Because I could clearly express military family concerns, I was viewed as the spokesperson for military families. After I began to work, doors were opened for other American civilians to work at the base. Previously, the hiring practices allotted non-military support positions to Spanish natives. American family members who had left jobs in the States and had come to Spain with their families, were left without jobs. They couldn't work on the military base or in the Spanish community, so they suffered financially. God used me to make a difference in hiring practices in Spain for American military family members – another pioneering effort.

Eventually, I was promoted to supervisor in the Navy Exchange Resale System, and finally I became Customer Service Manager. These platforms provided me with the opportunity to plan special events to address family concerns. I never dreamed that I would be a spokesperson for others in this way. The greatest joy was that I knew it was God who had orchestrated my job, my promotions, and everything else I had been able to do. Most significantly, I was given opportunities to speak with the Base Commander, the highest ranking official on the base.

As a result of my skills, I was appointed to various committees by the Base Commander to address issues on race relations, family matters, and employment practices. He began to trust me to address concerns not only for military families, but for the soldiers also. I planned events and entertainment for the soldiers, such as "soul night" and black history week activities. These activities helped develop a sense of community for the soldiers and their families. The success of these events caused the Base Commander to extend an open door policy for me. His support, cooperation and trust in me provided a platform to bring about changes. Civilian family member concerns were suddenly being heard. God used me to stand in the gap for our entire community. I also became the first non-military person and first black American citizen to work in the commissary grocery store, and during my spare time, I modeled for the Navy Exchange and a local boutique.

When our tour of duty ended in Spain, I asked God to lead us to the next place. Joe got his assignment papers and he was to be stationed in Norfolk, Virginia for his last tour of duty before retirement. We had hoped for an assignment closer to home in Georgia. We didn't want to be too far away from our parents who were now up in age. As far as I was concerned, Virginia was too far from Georgia, so I sought the Lord in prayer. After praying, I was prompted in my spirit to tell Joe that he shouldn't accept this assignment. He was to decline it because God had something better in store for us. With some hesitation, Joe put in a request for an alternative assignment. He had seen what God had done in the past through me and believed that God had spoken to me in this situation.

After Joe declined the assignment to Norfolk, he received an assignment to Whiting Field in Milton, near Pensacola, Florida. Excitement filled our hearts! This assignment would put us in the state adjoining Georgia and would make it possible for us to drive home in a few hours. The children would be able to see their grandparents more often and we could reconnect with family members we hadn't seen in three years while in Spain. God was so good to us! With each new victory, Joe and I realized more and more that God was definitely orchestrating our lives.

With new assignment papers in hand, we moved to Pensacola, Florida in June of 1974. We found housing immediately in newly developed military facilities at Corry Field. Since we were coming from overseas, we were number one on the housing list for placement. A friend of mine was working on the base at the Naval Air Station (NAS) in Pensacola and mentioned to her supervisor that I was coming there. He asked her to get in touch with me because he would have a vacancy and he wanted to consider me for the job. After the interview, I was hired on the spot. I became the manager of the convenience store at NAS Saufley Field. This was the first time a female had held this position. I began to see the pattern God was establishing in my life. It was clear to me that God was using me for His glory to open doors for others. I was in a position to help others. As the manager, I was responsible for hiring employees and was able to give many people opportunities for employment when none had existed before. Before I left, we had a significantly larger number of black employees than had ever been hired before. God had given me a position of authority where I could affect the lives of others. I was careful to remain humble. I never wanted to forget the many people who coached, encouraged and cheered me along the way.

We lived in Pensacola from 1974 to 1977. Since this was Joe's last assignment before retirement, we began planning for our last military move. Being gone from Georgia so long, we had really missed our families and wanted to move back home. While we were in Pensacola, my only brother David drowned tragically at 26 years old. From that time on, we yearned to be with the family. All these factors played a role in our decision to purchase a home in College Park, Georgia. We had promised the children we would be settled in a place where they could spend all four years of high school without having to change schools. We would live up to that promise in College Park.

Moving back to Georgia within close range of my hometown would be great for the children; however, I had mixed emotions about going back and facing the people and the circumstances of my own background and the mistakes I'd made. I was concerned about what people would think of me. Would they remember that I was a high school dropout, unwed mother and homeless, or would they want to know all of the wonderful things God had done in my life since leaving home? The fear of going back began to make me feel sad. Even though many benefited from my accomplishments everywhere I had lived since leaving Georgia, the local people had no idea what the Lord had done in my life. The Word of God says "a prophet is without honor in his own hometown (John 4:44)." I found this to be true.

In spite of my anxiety, the day came when we were back in our hometown and I was happy to be home. We arrived in the summer of 1977 and moved into our newly acquired home. We enrolled the children in public school, and they were excited because they had never attended a public school before. After helping us get settled in the house, Joe went back and remained in Florida until his retirement in December.

Maintaining two households was challenging, but God's grace was sufficient. God had prepared me for local employment by allowing me to develop skills in customer service. My customer service experience, ability to communicate effectively, and excellent references gave me an edge when I applied for jobs. I worked two jobs for the Christmas season at Sears and J.C. Penney's. God's favor allowed me to get into the work force quickly.

After working the Christmas season in department stores, I wanted a permanent job with benefits. In February of 1978, something inside compelled me to go through the telephone directory and call various Federal agencies to see if there were any job vacancies. I contacted the United States Department of Agriculture (USDA), Forest Service, and was offered a temporary job that later became permanent. Initially, I worked in the Office of Planning and Budget, Personnel Fiscal and Accounting, Fire and Lands Division. While working for USDA, I received special recognition and numerous merit awards because of my work on regional committees.

Throughout my life, God spoke to me about many things because I always sought Him in prayer and desired to hear His voice. I was willing to share the response I got from Him with those around me. What appeared like great wisdom to some was the voice of God working through me. God can and will use anyone as long as they ask, seek and knock. He wants to bless us and he often blessed me and my family greatly because of our asking.

Even before I had a full understanding of God, He was at

work on my behalf. I was seven months pregnant when I met Joe. Later, God revealed to me that Joe would be my husband, and that he would be a preacher. Since 1962 when this revelation came, no matter where we lived I would always tell our friends, "Joe is going to preach one day." It didn't matter that he was singing in nightclubs at the time. I didn't care that people would dispute my word or doubt what I said. Back then, I thought it would happen quickly because God had spoken it to me. I didn't realize how much of an influence I would have to be in my husband's life, and what changes he would have to make before becoming who God destined him to be, but I consistently spoke what God promised me for 17 years before it finally came to pass.

Joe was enthusiastic about music and he had a great singing voice. It was hard for him to resist the temptation to become a rhythm and blues artist. When the opportunity came for him to be considered for a contract with Motown, I reminded him, "You can't do that; you're going to preach the Word of God and sing praises to Him only!" He seemed disappointed, but obviously, he also knew that he was to preach and sing to the glory of God.

Our lives were not necessarily a testimony of where we were going with God, because while Joe was in the military neither of us attended church as regularly as we did when we were back home. Nevertheless, we always found a way for our children to be in church. Upon arriving in Georgia, I knew we needed to do everything we could to please God.

After settling in the Atlanta area, I enrolled Joe in Carver Bible Institute. I knew what God was about to do in his life, so

I obeyed His voice. For 17 years, I confessed Joe's calling to the ministry, and it was finally manifested. Shortly after entering Carver in the winter of 1978, Joe accepted his call to the ministry. Eventually, he completed his bachelor's degree in Biblical Studies at Beulah Heights Bible College (now Beulah Heights University) as a magna cum laude honor graduate. No one could have been more proud than I was when Joe was licensed in May of 1978 and ordained in November of 1978 at our home church in Griffin. In December of 1979, my husband was accepted as pastor of our church where he served faithfully for 17 years until he went home to be with the Lord.

From this and other experiences, I learned that God wants us to stay faithful to the vision and the Word He has placed in our hearts. Many times when God promises us something, He delivers it in his own time; it could be a few days, weeks or even years after we expect it. We have to remember that it's through faith and patience that we inherit the promise (Hebrews 6:12).

God had consistently shown me favor in every area of my life: He had blessed me with a wonderful husband; had supernaturally given me several jobs that I otherwise would not have received; had provided the best possible house situation in Spain, had sent neighbors to help me with my children, and had given us favor with military job assignments. I couldn't imagine what else God had in store for me, but the blessings continued to come.

When our youngest daughter, Tina, was 13 years old, we had another son. Even though we never anticipated another child, we were very happy because we knew he was sent from God. We named him Joseph Ken Harris. He was a bundle of joy and brought us so much happiness. His siblings saw him as *their* baby. They practically took him over. His grandparents showered him with much love and affection. He was the last grandchild in his generation and everyone wanted to spoil him. It was all we could do to keep him on the straight and narrow path.

When Ken was 11 months old, he became very sick and was diagnosed with viral croup. Thirty days later, after a trip to the emergency room, we came back home with our son with a tracheotomy tube in his throat that became a permanent fixture for the next three and a half years. Eventually, I had to quit my job to stay home and take care of Ken. We prayed and often confessed the Word for Ken's healing. We even taught him to lay hands on himself and confess healing for his body. We were a people of faith and we knew that God would move because of our faith. We had seen him move mountains in our lives before, and we knew He was faithful to watch over His Word to perform it. There were many trying and difficult times, but God heard our prayers and supernaturally healed Ken in the operating room at Egleston Children's Hospital in Atlanta in June of 1985.

After seeing God work miracles in my life repeatedly, I began to seek Him even more. I remembered how many times God had revealed things to me. As I listened more attentively, He spoke to me more readily. My spiritual eyes were becoming more sensitive to what God was doing. I began to see that God was always there orchestrating the circumstances of my life, rescuing me from dangers and moving me toward His will. I remembered five serious auto accidents where my cars were totaled and because of God's hand on my life, I was always rescued. No doubt, I had a work to do for the Lord and my life was not my own; it belonged to God.

In May of 1994, about two years before my husband's death, I was the first African American female licensed to minister in a historical church in the city of Griffin. Joe was very proud of me, but unfortunately, he did not live to see me flourish in the ministry. Reflecting on the loss of my husband makes me realize that losing him shaped the very foundation of my Christian faith.

Before Joe's death, it seemed that the favor and miracles I had experienced in my life were not as apparent to me. Many of the events that took place in my life and the people who influenced me, prove that God has always looked out for me. I will never forget my school teachers, Mrs. Margaret Kendall, Mrs. Josephine Johnson, and Mrs. Patricia Head who showed me that life could be better, my friend, Mrs. Chunk who let me live with her when I was put out by my mother, and Bert and her mother who took me in as a scared, pregnant teenager. Further, I am grateful for the traveling I have been able to do, the amazing children we have raised, and God's faithfulness to Joe and the ministry.

Despite the pain of losing Joe, I have made a decision to move forward. Yet, I sometimes wonder, "When will the difficulties of life end?" I often ask, "God, why are you allowing me to go through all of these hardships?" A still small voice in the back of my mind says, "If you had not had a broken heart, then you would not be as effective ministering to the brokenhearted; if you had not been a captive to something, then it would be difficult for you to set the captives free." These words, spoken quietly to my spirit, caused me to rejoice. My response is, "Lord, I thank you for the ministry of healing, reconciliation and liberty for your people! Let me minister well!"

The hardships still come and the blessings still flow. Living without Joe – his covering, his assistance, his support, and his love – has caused me to really appreciate the small miracles of daily life, the favor that comes with loving and serving an all powerful and all knowing God. Sometimes we fail to thank God for the everyday miracles and we fail to thank people in our lives for the small deeds of kindness they do for us. I have learned to appreciate both and to declare that everyday miracles are happening for me. I have learned to declare, "Every day of my life I see miracles." Miracles were and are still being manifested consistently. Here are just some of the miraculous incidents that have occurred in my life:

- While employed with the Federal government, I was nominated as Federal Employee of the Year.
- I received the United States Office of Personnel Management National Director's Award.
- In the summer of 1997, I became a student at Beulah Heights Bible College, my husband's alma mater. As a fringe benefit of Joe's military career, my tuition was paid in full.
- My son was able to attend and graduate from Landmark Christian School after his father's death due to the generosity of an anonymous donor who paid for his last two years of high school and his senior expenses.

- In 1997, I was a special guest at President Clinton's Inauguration in Washington, D.C.
- I have been able to minister throughout the United States, in Trinidad, Germany, Kenya, South Africa, Spain, Morocco, South America, Ghana, Guatemala, and Mexico.
- I have consistently received financial blessing from others. On four occasions, I have been given checks for $5,000.
- In 1999, Dr. Douglas Chatham, then Director of the Biblical Studies Department at Beulah Heights Bible College hired me to serve as his assistant.
- I became the first female Elder of the International Minister's Association (I.M.A.) at Beulah Heights University.
- In 1998, I established New Generation Christian Fellowship Church in Griffin.
- In 1999, I listed the home Joe and I had purchased in College Park for sell. After being on the market for one day, one visitor saw it and made me an offer. Within two days, we agreed upon a contract and the house was sold in 30 days.
- In 1999, I purchased a home that had been under contract with someone else, but God worked it out so I could buy it.
- In 2005, New Generation Christian Fellowship Church purchased a building and 3.75 acres of land valued at over $300,000.
- In 2005, I became the first female appointed to posi-

tion of District Director/Overseer of the Full Gospel Baptist Fellowship in Georgia.

- I have had the opportunity to appear and serve as co-host on local, national and international radio and television.
- Our New Generation Christian Fellowship Church Choir, Anointed Voices, was granted favor with a studio and released a recording. Additionally, Ken, my youngest son, released a CD called, "My Appointed Time"
- On a mission's trip to Kenya, Africa, I met former President Moye of Kenya.
- On another mission's trip to Kenya, I had lunch with the mayor and city officials of Nakurua.
- I have taken two trips to Jerusalem where I was able to visit many of the sites where biblical events took place.
- I ministered with Marilyn Hickey and her team in Morocco, Casa Blanca, Barcelona and Guatemala.
- I was blessed to have lunch with the Governor of Georgia.
- I have been a special guest on Trinity Broadcasting Network (TBN) and Atlanta TV 57.
- I have been the recipient of several all expense paid trips, including two trips to Hawaii and two to Las Vegas, Nevada.

There is never a day in my life that God does not show divine favor and provide supernatural blessings. I marvel at how He took someone like me who was born out of wedlock and grew up poverty-stricken in a small country town, to places I had only dreamed about. In spite of my mistakes and short-comings, He has truly made room for me among kings, presidents of countries, public figures and renowned educational and Christian leaders! I've discovered that when the favor of God is on your life, it's like an umbrella that covers and protects you.

I can honestly declare that no amount of exposure to prestigious people in high places will make me forget my roots and the God who took me from the pit to the palace. When I return home from one of my trips to Africa, Europe or South America, I like to revisit the farmland where I grew up. Seeing the vast wooded areas where I used to chop cotton always keeps me humble. I often tell my children about my challenging childhood and how God brought me to where I am today. I have purposed in my heart to make sure that my children, grandchildren, and everyone else knows of the goodness of God, the favor that rests upon my life and what favor they can have if they are obedient to His Word. To God be the glory for the great things he has done!

LIFE GOES ON

Aſter my husband's death, I was tossed back and forth by the surging waters of life, but I finally surfaced on the other side of the storm. As with natural storms like hurricanes and tornadoes, when basic components of our lives are disturbed or destroyed, eventually we have to deal with the damage, pick up the pieces and move on with life. Even though it is difficult, it can be done. I had to *decide* to move on. After forgiving people I thought mistreated me, and forgiving myself for the mistakes I made, I have learned to trust people again. No matter what happens in my life, I know God never leaves me.

Since Joe's death, I have had to allow the strength and boldness that God placed in my heart as a small child to emerge and be a positive influence rather than a negative one in my life. The same personality traits and characteristics that we are born with and that further develop during our formative years are what we need to achieve our purpose in life. God gives us the gifts and tools we need to fulfill our destiny.

Since coming out of this dark period of life, I have seen many things happen that I never imagined or thought possible before. I started a church that is growing and thriving, established a new home for myself, made many new faithful friends, and foremost, I have traveled the world ministering to brokenhearted people. God has shown me that I should not be afraid to face whatever He brings to my life because I can triumph. A positive attitude and a firm decision are prerequisites to achieving victory after a tragedy. We must decide how we will allow the experience to shape and influence our lives. In preparing to move on after Joe's death, I took several actions to ensure that I learned from the experience.

Maintaining Memory

Some people advise that one should forget about the lost loved one and simply move on, clearing all memories out of their home and heart and closing that chapter of life. From my experience, this is ill advice. We have to establish and maintain healthy memories of the loved one who played a significant role in our lives. Although death is final in the sense that we will not see our loved one again in this existence, we cannot pretend that they were not important to us. We should make every effort to preserve the great memories we have and the influence they had on us, and our family members, especially our children.

My children and I have done several things to celebrate

Joe's life. Initially, we established a scholarship fund at his home church. Later, we presented the church with an oil portrait in memory of his 17 years of service as pastor. In addition, we furnished a room in his honor at Beulah Heights University, his alma mater. Sometimes on special occasions, we place flowers on his grave; however, we do not linger at the gravesite because it can cause sadness. Since family dinners were our specialty, from time to time we visit Joe's favorite restaurant during the holidays and remember the happy times spent with him. We talk about Joe fondly, remembering his stories, funny expressions, and sense of humor. I recognize how important it is for my children to keep their dad in their hearts, even if I establish another male relationship.

Further, I made a shadow box with some of Joe's personal objects that I will pass on to our oldest son. I made portraits of Joe's younger pictures and blessed each child with a copy. I am currently working on a picture album of our years together as a family. As I move forward, I will plant flowering shrubbery in the backyard as a memorial to him. In addition, I plan to take my wedding ring and our 25th year wedding anniversary ring and create a keepsake memory that will represent our years together.

In my own quiet time, I sometimes sort through my box of cards and letters received from him, and smile, cry, and laugh. Occasionally, I read his sermons. Joe was a great husband and father and will always be a part of who I am. My memories are sweet and I am thankful for the wonderful relationship we had together for 34 years. As a gift sent from God, the children and I will always love and remember him. While we must move on, we cannot pretend that the portion of our lives spent with Joe did not exist. We cannot wipe them out, but we can remember them fondly and positively.

Making Changes

Without Joe, I made many lifestyle changes. Foremost, I have become more independent, but when situations are too difficult for me to handle alone, I rely totally on God. Just to deal with the immediate loss of my husband and their father, the children and I settled into a routine to help each other. We visited and stayed in touch with each other on a regular basis and continued to get together for Sunday dinner.

Over ten years later, our lives have changed significantly. Ken, who was still living at home at that time, has completed high school, college and graduate school. He is currently working on a doctorate degree. Sonya is now an elder in the church, is still working hard as a government employee, has remarried and is investing great energy into raising her two sons, Matthew and Joshua. Tina now teaches at the University of Georgia and has written several books. Greg has since gotten married, and lives in Florida and still works as an Air Traffic Controller.

Even though I gradually made small changes in my own life, my first major change came in 1999 when Ken left for college. It seemed like a perfect time to break ties with the house my family had called home for most of our married life. Being in a new place, I was able to disconnect from the memory of my husband being in the physical surroundings. It was an opportunity to start fresh in a new home.

I found, however, that being alone after having a constant companion was not easy. At night when I was alone and heard noises in the house, I would recite: "God is my shield and buckler. He guides and protects me. He keeps me from all harm. His angels watch over me to keep me from danger. No harm can come to me because he watches over me!" Just knowing that God is there brings tremendous comfort.

When I felt lonely, which I still feel sometimes, I would say, "God will never leave me, nor forsake me. He comforts me. He accepts me as I am. He understands me like no one else. He is my light in the darkest moments. He is my joy and peace. He is the best friend I have ever had. With God on my side, I can stand through the storm and rain. I am protected in His arms and He covers me with His love." In such moments, I often think about the childhood song that I learned in Sunday school that sustained me several times before, "*Yes, Jesus loves me. Yes, Jesus loves me. Yes, Jesus loves me, for the Bible tells me so!*"

Letting Go of Material Things

One thing I found particularly difficult to do was to get rid of Joe's personal belongings, like his car, his truck, his clothes, books, and other items that brought fond memories of him. Years after his death, I was still surrounded by many of his personal items that reminded me of my loss. I could not release his truck or his car. Nevertheless, about five years after Joe's death, a family friend did some mechanical work on the truck. When he did the test drive, the truck caught fire and burned up. I was devastated and heart broken!

With his truck gone, I felt obligated to preserve his car. Each of the children wanted it; but I didn't give it to either of them. For ten years, I held onto the car. Then one Tuesday night while driving home from Minister's Meeting during a thunderstorm, I swerved to miss a tree limb that had fallen on the road, had an accident, and destroyed the car. Gradually, I began to see that I was substituting material things for Joe. I was emotionally tied to his personal belongings. His things had come to represent him. I was holding on to them and allowing them power over me. I believe these vehicle mishaps were God's way of telling me to let go of Joe's "things" and move on with my life. God was helping me in disguise. These actions were part of my emotional healing.

My emotional healing progressed significantly when I read a book about grief written by Martha Felker. In the book, she recommends that the grieving person prepare a plan of action to work their way out of grief. Keeping with her recommendation, I made my plan and decided to start the New Year in 2006 with a goal to put the past in perspective and face the future. I began letting go of many of Joe's personal belongings that I had held on to.

With God's help, I removed pictures and other memorabilia that stirred grief in me. I realized that I was continuing to grieve because I had surrounded myself with things that made me feel sorrow. Encouraged by my plan of action, I sorted through Joe's clothing and gave items to foreign students at Beulah Heights University. After I have compiled several memory books that I am still working on, I will give away any remaining items that may be useful to others. I will give some items to the children. I will donate many of his books to missionaries from Kenya and Beulah Heights University.

Finally, I gave the bedroom set I shared with Joe to our son, Ken, and replaced it with a new one. This deed represented the culmination of my marriage to Joe and my decision to move on with life.

All these actions will help finalize my grief and end my story. I have discovered that many times we tell our tales of woe to receive sympathy from others. Although I never thought of myself as one seeking attention, now I realize that sometimes I have told people my story out of my loneliness and pain. It brought comfort to me for others to know the difficulties I had experienced. As part of my healing, I have decided to stop retelling the stories of my pain unless it is in the context of ministry where someone else can receive healing from their own pain.

An Open Door to a New Relationship

After cleaning out Joe's personal things and coming to grip with my own emotions, I have decided that I am ready for a new relationship. I have come to realize that remarriage is a possibility. God has helped me know, through examining my own life, ministry and feelings that I can love again. Remembering what Joe always said to me has also helped me. Periodically, he would say, "Mamie, I know you're ten years my junior. If anything happens to me, I want you to go on with your life. You have so much to offer. Some man would be honored to have you as a wife. You are one of a kind. You are intelligent, courageous, loving, giving, honest and trustworthy. You are a prize; a good catch!"

I realize how much I enjoyed marriage so I would consider marriage again if the circumstances and opportunity were to arise. In my own marriage, I enjoyed being a helpmeet for my husband and I would willingly serve in that capacity again. I had to get to a place of emotional health. Until I was fully healed, I was not ready to enter a new relationship. The healing process takes longer for some than for others.

Looking back, I realize that I could have dealt with my issues sooner had I made a concerted effort to move on. However, maybe I was wise not to move too quickly and begin thinking of a new relationship before I was emotionally ready. Personally, dating is not a concept that I fully understand or know how to deal with. I have asked the Lord to exclude me from dating. When, and if he has someone for me, I would rather that He orchestrate the details supernaturally without my having to go through the dating process.

Filling the Time

My life has always been a flurry of activities. Even when I worked a full time job, I was also busy taking care of the house, the children, giving ministry support, and working on committees and projects. After Joe's death, I made myself even busier to avoid being alone. I would over schedule activities and then exhaust myself trying to keep up with everything. Eventually, I would fall in the bed, thoroughly worn out and try to sleep it off. I was absorbed in ministry work, helping people, and looking for projects. These were cure alls for missing Joe. My calendar stayed full and I would add other activities regularly. With all that I participated in, I never attended a singles group. I felt like such a ministry would not address the concerns of a widow, and surely would not address the specific issues of a pastor's widow.

Keeping extraordinarily busy kept me from facing my own fears of being alone. It kept me from grieving *when* I should have and *how* I should have. Now that I've dealt with my pain, my goal is to move forward by learning to say, "No" when appropriate, and not feeling guilty about it. Life is too short to spend time obligated to things you don't really enjoy.

Preparing for a New Lifestyle

Any change made in our lifestyle requires effort and repetition until a new pattern of behavior is established. How am I preparing myself for my new lifestyle? First, I am on a journey to reduce the stress causing factors in my life. I have begun to exercise weekly and spend more quiet time with the Lord. I am practicing relaxation methods, drinking more water and making and keeping health care appointments. In addition, I am focusing more on maintaining a healthy diet and lifestyle, and pursuing things that will make my life more enjoyable. I enjoy meeting new people and find that it is easier for me to make male friends; however, the greatest challenge in this area is that some men are reluctant to have a friendly conversation with a pastor. God will have to work this out for me.

Instead of using constant activity to fill my life as an

avoidance tactic, I have made a list of things that I plan to do. My list has been placed in a highly visible area, the front of the refrigerator, so that I'm reminded daily of the commitments I have made. Currently, I am working on getting my life more organized, using my time more wisely, setting daily goals, spending more time with the Lord, and seeking to walk in obedience to Him. My prayer is, "Lord, help me to stay focused on one task at a time until it is completed, then move on to another task." I have decided not to let the telephone hinder my progress in moving on with my life. It had become my constant companion because of loneliness. I used it to avoid being alone, to keep from thinking about my situation, and from facing my fears. I know that eventually, we have to face reality before we can process how we will deal with it.

Continue Moving Toward Your Purpose

If my husband had not passed away, I often wonder what I would be doing today. It is impossible to know how our lives would turn out if situations and circumstances were different. I believe that only God knows this, however, I do believe that as long as we are willing to follow His lead, somehow He works things out so we can achieve our purpose. God is sovereign and He ultimately controls everything, even though we have freedom of choice. I believe that I was destined to start a church and minister to broken-hearted people. The story of how I came to minister to people all over the world unfolded slowly.

In February 1987, I answered the call to minister to women by establishing the Victorious Women's Fellowship. This fellowship of women met on a regular monthly basis. I instituted an annual retreat where women could come together and share, hear, and receive from the Lord in a quiet, prayerful environment. In 1990, I acknowledged my calling to ministry and was licensed as a minister in May of 1992. I was ordained in May of 1996 at our home church in Griffin, GA where my husband Joseph Harris was pastor.

All these things took place prior to Joe's death. It seemed that God was setting the stage for what He wanted me to do in the future. I did not know it at the time; however, God always works behind the scenes preparing us for what is to come even when we are totally in the dark regarding His plan.

My experience has taught me that as a woman of God, I had to find my place after my husband's death. When one determines their gifts and callings, then they are obligated to put them to work for the Lord. It becomes our responsibility to trust God and allow Him to provide a platform for our gifts. God would not give you gifts and then ask you to hide them under a bushel. They are to be used for His glory, regardless of life's circumstances. Each of us is a unique individual whom God called before the foundation of the earth. Our responsibility is to live according to His purpose. A spouse cannot do that for us. A parent cannot do that for us. A pastor, a friend or anyone else can't push us into our destiny. We must know who we are in Christ, and this Christ-centered self-confidence will be essential to realizing our dreams.

I knew without a doubt that God had called me to minister to the broken-hearted and to set the captive free, according to Luke 4:18-19. After my husband's death, and finding out that I couldn't serve in a leadership role at our home church, I yielded to my passion for the ministry. Forsaking a lucrative 18-year career with the Federal government, I took a leap of faith and decided to totally trust God to fulfill the call upon my life. God gradually led me to my purpose, step by step.

The year after my husband's death, through Mamie Harris Outreach Ministry, I began holding fellowship services at Ashford Place Apartment on Carver Road in Griffin, GA. In doing so, God gave me a vision to reach the lost at any cost, and to train and empower believers to develop and become an effective part of the five-fold ministry team, according to Ephesians 4:10-11. I had faith in God that I would receive the promise, that the people would come. I stepped out on God's promise and the people came and continue to come.

In the fall of 1997, New Generation Christian Fellowship was conceptualized. Mamie Harris Outreach Ministry began having worship services at what was then, Faith Temple Assembly of God Church, 1344 North 9th Street, Griffin, GA., with seven faithful and committed believers. God revealed to me then that this building would be our permanent place of worship. In February of 1998, New Generation was birthed, formally established as a church body, and was certified in the State of Georgia as a 501(c) (3), Non-profit Organization.

From February 1999 thru January, 2003, New Generation relocated three times to reflect the continued growth of our congregation. During this time of transition, I was ordained as an Apostle by Bishop Keith Ramdass in 2002. While serving as pastor, I have in turn ordained many to the ministry as elders, ministers, and deacons.

Finally, in January of 2005, seven years after New Generation was started, with faithful, consistent prayer and standing firm in faith, God brought the church full circle. The property once owned by Faith Temple was purchased by New Generation Christian Fellowship Church. The church is currently located at this site at 1344 North 9th Street, in Griffin, Georgia – the place that God said would be our permanent home. What an awesome God we serve! All Glory goes to Him.

Build Your Legacy

Planting a church or starting a ministry is very challenging, but if God leads you, He will bless the work of your hands. I really had no plans to start a church; God just worked it out that way. It was a difficult task for me as a woman because many men thought that I was outside the will of God. Even men shy away from starting a church because of the financial challenges, the difficulty of attracting and maintaining a committed team of leaders and members, and the uncertainty of whether it will last. With God's help, I was able to plant a successful church.

A MESSAGE TO HURTING PEOPLE

Since becoming a widow after a 34-year marriage, rediscovering my identity and my purpose in life has been challenging. My husband's death forced me to look inward, to reexamine my life, and assess my purpose. This has been difficult, primarily because I was under constant scrutiny of others – particularly Christian brothers and sisters. In spite of everything, God has been faithful. He has brought me through the valley of darkness, shed light on my experience, and given clarity to my purpose. From my own experience, I have learned many lessons that may help others face and overcome pain, and live a healthy purpose-filled life after the loss of a loved one, especially a spouse.

Lesson 1: Take Time to Grieve.

Grief is a very complex emotion. It takes place in stages and cannot be squelched. Grief-stricken people need time to recover. I didn't really take time to grieve after my husband's death. Out of my desire to help others, I put my own grieving process on the back burner by trying to be strong for my children. Being a source of strength and encouragement for the church body, I focused on helping them transition to a new pastor. I thought time would heal my wound. Understandably, I carried my grief for a long time. Finally, I had to sort out my emotions, release my own pain, and decide that even without Joe, I could be happy, and feel whole.

In retrospect, it's apparent that I boxed God and myself in by deciding that I had to be strong for others. The standard of behavior I set for myself was hard to meet. Everyone marveled at how well I seemed to adjust to Joe's death. Clearly, they had no idea how heartbroken I was. In public, I was strong and unshaken, but in the privacy of my home, I was the lonely, grieving widow who no longer had a place in her church. I was the former "First Lady" whom the church did not help financially. I lived in what seemed like a semi-conscious state, living two separate lives. During the day, I did the things I needed to do, but at night, I would slip into the bathroom and cry. In my room, I would bury my head in my pillow and cry quietly for fear that Ken might hear me and get upset. I needed to release my pain. I wanted to rant, rave and scream from the top of my lungs that I was hurting, that my husband was dead, that I loved him and missed him. It seemed no one really understood what I was going through.

I didn't know whom to trust with my deepest fears. The pain and frustration I felt was bottled up inside me. I couldn't find a way to freely express my emotions. From my early childhood, I had learned to survive by not crying. I learned to be strong and courageous, to put on a strong face and deal with the hardships of life. Therefore, I was strong. I *had* to be strong! It was all I knew. Yet, in my heart I cried, "God, please help me be free!" I need to cry loud and hard!" I wanted to yell and scream! I needed to let go of the heavy weight that sat upon my chest and shoulders day and night. I couldn't get rid of it. As a minister, I felt like I should have reacted differently. I felt guilty for carrying such grief around with me. I knew Joe was in a great place of peace and love, and I knew death would eventually come to all of us. I asked myself, *"Why can't I accept Joe's death and move on?"*

For years, I carried around embedded pain. Joe's death was still keen in my memory and in my heart. Finally, I came to realize that spiritual maturity does not result in perfect behavior. Ministers sometimes forget that they are human, too. No matter what we know about God, none of us can predict how we will react to the death of our spouse or loved one, especially when it comes suddenly and unexpectedly.

My heart's desire is to share my experience to help others. Because of my own mistakes, I know how important it is to take time to grieve. When children are involved, it's all right to help them grieve, but spouses also need to express their own sorrow. None of us is perfect. We cannot become overly concerned about others that judge and criticize our reactions.

———

129

Each person experiences and releases pain in a unique way. If you are in ministry and used to helping others, there comes a time when you need help, and it's okay to receive that help from others. There is a time to give and a time to receive. In times of need, relax and receive, even from your children. They may have an easier time grieving if you express your grief because children sometimes grow closer to their parents when they share grief.

Lesson 2: Take Care of Your Physical Body

After Joe's death, I ate very little. I felt physically weak and spent many sleepless nights, tossing and turning and thinking of my life, the children, and the ministry. I quietly shed tears wondering what would happen to the church. The physical strain began to take a toll on my body. I was constantly worn down and exhausted. I needed to have a good crying session. I had suffered such physical, emotional and verbal abuse as a child that I couldn't openly express my emotions. I convinced myself that if others saw me cry they would think I was weak and spineless. As a child, others were quick to call you a wimp if you backed down or showed emotion, so I compensated by being tough. I was relentless and would not back down. With this pattern of behavior established in my life, I buried my grief.

Grief was overtaking me, and I didn't take proper care of my physical body. Had I known what I know now, I would have at least done physical exercise. A good workout can relieve the body of stress, clear out the lungs and allow for free breathing. Exercise would have helped me deal with my emotional anxiety. One can often think more clearly after physical exertion. It's a great way to reinvigorate your physical body and emotional state of being. I recommend it.

Lesson 3: Get Rid of Too Many Physical Reminders

Living around Joe's personal belongings on a daily basis caused the grief to surface regularly and kept me feeling sad. I was constantly reminded of him. His favorite Bible was still laying on a stand in our bedroom. Often, I would pick it up and the scent of his fragrance, and his handwriting in the margins would cause me to grieve. I would stare into space and ask God, *"Can Joe see me? Why did he have to go so soon?"* Walking around in the bedroom, I would see his favorite chair, the remote control holder, the caps he collected, his library of books, and his cars, all constant reminders that he was gone. The things he used to do went undone. He had taken great pride in cleaning the cars every week and keeping them filled with gas. I had depended on him to take care of my car. I wondered, *"Who will take care of my car?"* I didn't know anything about getting oil changed, car maintenance, or service warranties. I just drove the car and Joe did the rest. My life had been turned upside down and I needed help. I am reminded of the first time I went to the gas station. As I drove up to the pump, I was thinking about Joe. I pulled the handle off the hook and tried to pump the gas, but it didn't work. After several unsuccessful attempts, tears began filling my eyes. All of a sudden, a man came over and said,

"Ma'am, you have to lift the lever. Seeing my tears he asked, "Are you okay?" I thanked him and replied, "Yes. I'm fine." This experience represented a new lifestyle that I didn't want to embrace. I was not prepared for it.

Lesson 4: Accept Encouragement From Whoever Gives It.

During the grieving period, one should not expect to receive encouragement, inspiration and blessings from the same people they have helped. As ministers, we often help others, especially our ministry peers thinking that they will be there for us. We cannot predict *where* our blessings will come from, or *how* God will heal and restore us. I expected church members and pastors we had helped to be there for me when Joe died. This was not necessarily the case. Out of my disappointment, I may have pulled away from them, unknowingly.

After seeing very few church people, ministers and friends respond as I expected them to, I became angry and sarcastic in my spirit. Sometimes people would say to me, "I know how you feel!" I would think, "No, you don't!" If they said, "He's in a better place." I'd think, *"Then why don't you want to do die!"* Others would say, "Let me know if there is anything I can do." I thought, *"That's a good indication that you will do nothing!"* Several said, "You know, it could be worse. At least you have your children. You *will* see him again." This made me angry, and I'd think, *"Do you think that stops the pain of losing my husband?"* I never actually spoke these words, but I did speak sharply to close family and friends. I now realize that my anger was not directed at them, but was my reaction to Joe's death. Most counselors will tell you that anger is one of the stages of grief. I knew everyone meant well, but I only heard what was said after it was filtered through my pain.

Lesson 5: Trust God, Not People

Through my experience, God showed me that instead of having expectations of others based on what we have done for them, we must simply trust Him. Whatever we do, we are to do it as unto the Lord, and then He makes provision for us in His own way. It's my experience that often God meets our needs and blesses us through unexpected sources. One day I was sitting home alone feeling deserted, abandoned and rejected. I thought, *"Where are all the people who used to be around when Joe was alive."* I needed encouragement. During my questioning thoughts, suddenly, the doorbell rang. I got up and went to the door. To my surprise, there stood a deliveryman with a beautiful floral arrangement from Dr. Joseph and Marjanita Ripley from the Body of Christ Church, in Fayetteville (now located in College Park, GA). What a joy it was to know that they were sensitive to the Holy Spirit. They were distant acquaintances, not a couple I had spent much time with, or even talked to on a regular basis. God always knows just *when* and *how* to touch the hearts of people who will then, touch your heart. He used them to bless me. I learned how important it is to receive from whoever God sends to minister to you. He hears and answers prayer, not always the way we expect. We must trust that when we plant seeds of faith, they will grow and produce a harvest. It may come from many different sources, as God wills.

Lesson 6: Prepare for Retirement

When one is called to pastor a church, he or she must inquire about a retirement fund for themselves and the opportunity for their family to become the beneficiary upon their death. Many churches today have benefits packages for pastors. If a plan is offered, it is important to understand under what circumstances the spouse and family will receive benefits upon the death of the pastor. Also, It's significant to know how many years the pastor must serve before benefits are given. Even pastors and ministers may find it difficult to talk of their own death, but it's important for all parties to make preparations. It saves everyone from having to discuss sensitive matters during an already difficult period of grief.

From my own ministry experience, I've learned that pay and benefits packages range from small monthly salaries with no benefits to huge salaries with extensive benefits such as paid vacations, retirement funds, life and health insurance, housing allotments, telephone and car expenses. No two churches offer the same benefits. Each minister must be led by the Holy Spirit when accepting an offer; however, they must have a clear understanding of what the benefits are, and how and under what circumstances they will be given. A clearly written and understood agreement with the church will help the pastor and his wife prepare for retirement and survivor benefits. Even when the church makes provisions for the pastor, it's still wise to talk to a financial planner and adviser to get ideas of how to plan for one's own financial future and that of their family in the event of the pastor's death.

Lesson 7: Discover Your Own Identity

When the pastor of a church dies, the wife is no longer considered the "First Lady" of the church as she is often called in some denominational churches. She must either reestablish identity within the congregation and church family, or go wherever the Lord leads.

Of course, I didn't expect that my husband would die suddenly, so I had no understanding of what my role in the church would be after his death. I simply had not thought about it. Even though the church my husband pastored had been founded by his grandfather. I realized after some heartbreaking meetings and experiences that I no longer had a place there. I did not have an assigned ministry role outside of supporting my husband. I was no longer "First Lady" and realized that members saw me as the "Pastor's wife." My ministry work was viewed as part of my husband's role. I was surprised at this discovery because I had operated as a minister in my own right. In spite of some who disapproved of "women preachers", I knew God had called me to the prophetic ministry had given me the gift of administration, which I willingly used to support the church and my husband as pastor.

When Joe died, I went from one whose opinion counted to someone who was ignored. I thought people really loved and cared for me and valued my ministry. It was devastating to know that they only saw me as a helper to my husband. All of a sudden, I had no place in the church family. This situation made relationships with many members a bit awkward.

Since Joe's passing, I've thought a lot about the term "First

Lady." I understand the concept; however, the term may be limiting, and does not give credence to the gifts and callings of the pastor's wife. The implication for me was that since I was no longer the "First lady"; I was no longer a viable minister. For wives who only view their role as "the pastor's wife," the term may not be a problem. For others who are involved in the five-fold ministry, the title mayis limiting. I advise women not to be trapped or limited by the title such "First Lady." If a woman is a minister in her own right, then she should be called Minister or Pastor.

When the pastor of a church passes away, many people will take on a new attitude about the surviving spouse. If a church has not had a pastor die while in service, they may have no idea how to deal with the surviving spouse. With no benefits package stipulating survivor benefits, the church may do nothing for the remaining spouse. Such was the case with me. In addition, church leaders may be concerned for the financial security of the church and be insensitive to the financial needs of the surviving spouse. Furthermore, when the pastor and his wife operate in a team ministry approach, the loss of the pastor may stifle ministry opportunities for the widow, and eliminate or severely reduce their income. This creates a great hardship for the surviving spouse and family.

The lack of a benefits package with specific provisions spelled out creates a controversial situation that can create hostility where church members may take sides. Surviving spouses of a pastor should expect relationships with some members to change, some positively and some negatively. The death of your spouse will reveal those who are sincere in their relationships and those who are not.

Lesson 8: Release Yourself from Dead Relationships

My greatest pain was walking through the doors of the church on Sunday morning and hearing someone else preach. It was a constant reminder that Joe would never preach in a pulpit again. I hurt. I wanted people to embrace me and comfort me. Not many stepped up to the plate from the household of faith. In fact, most of my support came from individuals who were not pastors and ministry leaders. I wondered, "Where were all of Joe's sons in the ministry and their wives who had showed up the night he died. I felt empty and alone. I didn't know that God had new friends lined up for me. He wanted me to trust Him, not people. There were genuine, kind-hearted people who knew nothing of my experience that would become my support team. I had to let go of dead relationships, release people from my expectations and let go of disappointments.

With the release of dead relationships, God brought people into my life that helped me survive. A few faithful friends remained and some of our military friends reconnected with me during my crises. Some were local, but many lived out of town. One of my dearest friends, Dr. Odell Tumblin, a minister from Alabama, was there for me when Joe went to be with the Lord. Alma Lowry, my best friend from Pittsburgh, was with me through the entire experience of Joe's death and my transition afterwards.

Audrey Hughes from Birmingham was always a comfort and a prayer warrior for me. She spoke prophetic words into my life that lifted me up and made me know that God was still with me. Cynthia Graham from Florida and Gwen Austin from Birmingham stayed close by through all my difficulties. In addition, my friend Marian Corbin would drop by or call. God expanded my circle of friends. Each one brought their own unique personality and contribution to my life, and blessed me in their own way. When I sort through mounds of paper, I remember Brenda Chand from the acronym she shared with me, O.H.I.O. that stands for "only handle it once".

Dr. Douglas Chatham was, and still is, a constant source of support and prayer. He is like a father to me, and is in fact, my father in ministry. I rely on him for wisdom and spiritual guidance when I don't know who to turn to or what to do. God uses him to bless my life and my ministry. His wife Jackie has such a kind supportive spirit and is like a mother to me. They are truly God's servants.

Through all the shifting of relationships, I realize that it's important to have friends who understand and appreciate you for who you are. Different stages in life require different friends, and God brings individuals in our lives who serve a specific purpose for each stage of our journey. I have learned to accept those that He sends.

Lesson 9: Find Your Place in the World

My greatest spiritual concern was, "How do I move on in ministry without my husband?" I knew I was called of God to preach and teach. Joe was my covering, the one who helped make a way for me in ministry. When he was alive, I did not move outside of his covering, nor did I minister without his blessings. Now, he was no longer there to pray for my ministry work and me. I had to rely totally on the Lord and His guidance. I trusted God before; it's just that Joe was my human sounding board.

I felt compelled to continue in ministry; however, I had no plans to start a church. God just worked it out that way. God blessed my efforts and today we have a vital, growing church.

Being a pastor is a great responsibility, but being a female pastor carries with it an additional set of challenges. Every pastor needs a support system, a group of spiritually seasoned men and women of God, who will pray for, and mentor them in ministry. My first challenge as a female pastor came from men who don't believe that women should be pastors because they are not to have authority over men. As a result, I got no support from them. My support came from men and women who believed in my calling. Ultimately, I had to depend on God.

Additionally, as a single female pastor, I had no one with whom I could share my ideas. When Joe was a pastor, he would come home and talk through church problems and issues with me, and I would discuss ministry concerns with him. When one is a single pastor, there may not be another individual with whom you can share the joys and sorrows of ministry. When I come home from a mission's trip, I'd love to talk to someone about my experiences and the wonderful works of the Lord. That's a part of married life that I really miss. Joe and I would share and counsel with each other completely and honestly about church situations. Close friends can help fill the need for fellowship, but they can't take the place of a spouse.

Another concern I have as a female pastor is how to relate to and deal with men, not only those in ministry, but men in the congregation, and those who may approach you socially. I am committed to stay above reproach in every way, not allowing any one to deter me from the Lord's work. When I encounter men who reject my leadership because I'm a woman, I stand my ground with out being offensive. God knows my heart and my calling. He helps fight my battles. When difficulties arise in ministry, we are to seek His guidance and direction.

Lesson 10: Decide If You Will Consider Remarriage

The idea of remarriage is sometimes a difficult issue for people who were married many years and had a good relationship with their spouse. I recommend that one consider remarriage much sooner than I did. When a survivor is considerably young, God can and often does bless them with another spouse.

First, the grieving process must be complete. However, missing married life is not a sufficient reason to justify marriage again. Entering a new relationship or getting married too quickly may generate problems, especially if the survivor has not sufficiently grieved. Each person has to determine when and if he or she is ready for another spouse. Nevertheless, I recommend at least a year or two to grieve, recapture your identity as a single person, and reestablish your life.

It is especially important to wait before entering a relationship if you have young children at home. Children may find it difficult to accept someone else in your life. They may view the individual as someone trying to *replace* their father or mother, whichever the case may be. One must proceed delicately when introducing a person of the opposite sex to their children. Be sensitive to them; however, keep in mind that they will grow up and leave, and you will have to make your own life. Seek God on when and how to approach dating or remarriage.

Lesson 11: Don't Build Walls

Nehemiah was a wall builder who did so under the wisdom and guidance of the Lord. (Nehemiah 3, 4) We have to know when to build walls and when to tear them down. As far as relationships are concerned, I found myself building a wall of protection around my heart to avoid dealing with male relationships. This emotional wall was detrimental to my developing a healthy relationship.

Since I have known the Lord, my desire has been to please Him. I realize that I feared someone taking advantage of my vulnerability, so I became defensive. I felt lonely, yet I didn't want to become open prey for attracting the wrong type of person, male or female. I had to become prepared both emotionally and mentally to handle the situation in the event someone was attracted to me. God has shown me that He is truly my helper in every area of life. I just need to let him help me. Fortunately, I have not received unwanted advances from men as some widows have said they receive. Because of prayer, I believe God put a shield of protection around me to allow me to heal and stay focused on him.

Lesson 12: Revere God

I thank God that today I am enjoying what He has called me to do, which is to minister to broken-hearted people. Even though there have been detours, He has opened many doors for me to move into my destiny. During his life, Joe's vote of confidence kept me afloat, but his death forced me into accepting my calling and purpose. God has called me to the nations. *"Ask of Me, and I will give You the nations as Your inheritance, and the uttermost parts of the earth as Your possession"* (Psalm 2:8). I have come from a poor, lonely, abused child, through the safety net of my husband, and have finally landed squarely in the arms of a loving God who has become my protection, my guide, my comforter, and my deliverer. God is always faithful, and will always make a way. Each new day brings an opportunity to see the mighty works of the Lord and experience untold miracles. My heart is fixed, and I have set my face like a flint, ready to face life with renewed hope and the joy of the Lord. You can do the same.

In His unconditional love, God used a simple childhood song that I learned in Sunday school to save me over and over again:

Yes, Jesus loves me.

Yes, Jesus loves me.

Yes, Jesus loves me, for the Bible tells me so.

Remember, Jesus loves *you*, too!

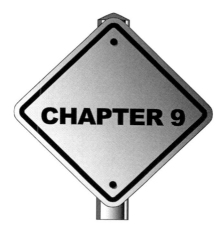

THE CHILDREN SPEAK

THE HARRIS LEGACY

As the eldest child, I love being a part of the Harris family and cherish the family values my parents instilled in us. We were taught fairness and equality in the midst of a loving, disciplined, and caring home.

As I reflect on what it has meant to be born into my family, the common thread that seemed to tie my memories together was the sense of fairness and equality for which our parents always fought. They provided us with a loving, disciplined, and caring home, yet, they seemed to be destined to a greater work that influenced many lives, other than our own. As pastors, they sought to help those who were forgotten, less fortunate, treated unfairly and disregarded.

I have vivid memories of the 1960s when we moved from Georgia to Michigan. I remember long walks to school with two hard-boiled eggs to keep me warm and learning to ice skate on the frozen ponds on Selfridge Air Force Base. In the midst of racial tensions, we were taught to love all of God's children regardless of his or her race, color, creed, or religion. Even though the country was riddled with racial injustices, involvement in war and internal struggles, my life was carefree, insulated by the safety and comfort of a home filled with love. No matter what was going on outside of our closed doors, we had each other, and our beliefs and principles.

After the turbulent times of the 1960s, we were stationed in Rota, Spain, where we grew together as a family. The challenge of living in a foreign country brought us closer together. In addition to loving one another, we learned to play as siblings and to respect our parents and all adults, no matter what. To preserve our sense of family, we had prayer and dinners together every night at 6:00 PM, which gave us the chance to discuss our lives. We had plenty of peace and quiet time. In addition, we were blessed to learn the Spanish culture, heritage, and language through the relationships we established with Spanish friends and their families.

I will never forget going to the docks to buy fresh calamari, stomping grapes to make wine, and observing "The Running of the Bulls". These experiences gave all of us an appreciation for a culture that we otherwise would not have.

When we moved from Florida to Atlanta, Georgia, church became a great part of family life. We attended a church in Griffin, GA, which was founded by my great grandfather. After traveling around for many years, I wanted to be free to enjoy my teen years. However, our church life took precedence.

We would leave home early every Sunday morning, drive 35 miles to church and stay all day. As a teenager, I was not happy about the day's activities. For several years, this was a struggle for me.

After settling in Atlanta, several events caused our family bond to grow stronger. The birth and near-death experience of my younger brother gave all of us a new sense of the meaning of life. It was not about any of us individually but all of us collectively. All of us have made a lifetime commitment to the Lord and each other.

Although "Pops" (as I affectionately called Dad) has gone on before us, we will continue in his teachings to praise God, respect and honor our mother and help each other. After all, this is the Harris family legacy.

– Greg Harris

Unwavering Faith that Covers

My parents always displayed an abiding faith in God and taught us through their words and deeds how to walk with the Lord. It was their example that taught me to have unwavering faith in God regardless of my life circumstances. Many times, I saw situations and circumstances change because of their faith. Together, they seemed to move mountains. Not only did they believe wholeheartedly in the Word of God for their own lives, but they also displayed the same level of faith when operating in the church and ministering to others.

They were encouragers and always encouraged us to be

our best. They did everything they could for us. As children, we didn't always understand the importance of their ministry and career schedules, but they would give us as much time as they could. I am most amazed at how Mom and Dad always took care of our basic needs. We never lacked anything. While it is a parent's responsibility to feed, clothe, and house their children, being a parent myself now, I realize that doing this often becomes a challenge. Mom and Dad worked multiple jobs and thought of creative ways to meet our needs when funds were low. Since growing up, we have heard stories of how times were tough and our parents were concerned about bills, food, and other necessities, but that concern was never passed on to us. We knew that we had a loving home environment where our parents always loved and provided for us.

Growing up in a house filled with godly faith, we were taught love, responsibility, respect, compassion, and leadership. These Christian principles became the backbone of our spiritual growth and development as adults. At age 15, I entered the workforce, which allowed me to pay my own car note and insurance. Mom and Dad taught us that in order to get what we wanted in life we had to work hard. Personally, I learned not to expect someone else to meet my needs, but to pursue my dreams and goals with a plan of action.

Although I did not appreciate it then, I now value the structure and discipline that we learned from having daily chores; it taught us obedience to our parents and God, and respect for the home we were blessed with. In addition to a strong work ethic and a sense of responsibility, our parents also showed us love, compassion, and respect by helping us when we were in need. They made sure we learned to help ourselves first. They were there to help us, but not to take charge of our responsibilities. Specifically, they encouraged us to excel in areas where we had gifts and talents, and they tried to help us move toward God's plan for our lives.

Above everything else, Mom and Dad showed us how important it is to have a serious relationship with God. This included being serious about the call that was on our lives, as well as living our lives according to God's Word. Mom showed us what it meant to be a woman of faith, believing God for the impossible when everything around us said otherwise. When we felt unsure of things, both Mom and Dad reassured us that we could get through the large and small difficulties of life. Mom was faithful to remind us that God is our source, and that we cannot depend on others.

While our parents showed us the serious side of life, Dad had the uncanny ability of finding humor in small things. We were always sure to find him cracking a joke, telling stories, or doing something funny so he could see a smile on our faces, or maybe even hear a good, hearty laugh. We didn't realize it at the time, but his sense of humor was an important part of our family, a part we will always treasure.

Although Dad is no longer with us, he would be proud to know the love he showed his grandsons lingers on, and we are doing all that we can to fulfill his wish: to raise our families in the fear and admonition of God, just as he did. My two sons are often a challenge, but I have purposed to nurture them to be men of valor, honor, and integrity like their grandfather. The legacy of Dad's love for God and family will always be remembered.

Since Dad's death, I have found Mom's continued faith to be invaluable in my life and in her ministry. Over the years, I've witnessed her becoming softer, laughing more, and becoming more powerful and anointed in delivering the Word to God's people. She brings clarity and understanding to the Word that breaks yokes and sets captives free. More importantly, she is a woman of faith, which I truly admire. I have seen her walk in love in the midst of rejection. Not once, has she ever expressed fear or doubt; rather, she has shown unwavering faith and confidence in God, His plan and promises. As I lived through her dealing with the loss of Dad, I am amazed by the courage she has. Her trials and tests appeared to have ushered her into the supernatural anointing that rests upon her life. If I could only be half as great as she is as a courageous ambassador for Christ, I would truly be honored and humbled. As her daughter, friend, and church elder who has worked beside her in ministry, it is a blessing to be part of God's awesome plan for her life! I love you Mom.

– Sonya Crowder

Precious Memories

I'm sure we've all heard the saying, "You don't miss a good thing until it's gone." Unfortunately, there are times when this homage to something great in our lives is spoken when we lose a loved one. While this in no way describes my love and feelings for my father, it's the small things in life that remind me of the loving household Mom and Dad created for us while growing up.

Mom and Dad had a love and passion for God, family, and the church, and as any pastor's child knows, this can be a difficult balancing act to manage. My siblings and I witnessed the hard work and dedication that came with being the proverbial "First Family", which challenged us to value and appreciate those quiet family times that we treasure to this day. Being in ministry is a high calling with minimal earthly rewards; however, from my parents, I have learned that the greatest reward comes from knowing that you are walking in obedience to what God has called you to do. There have been many times when one of them was called away to pray for a church member, attend a funeral, counsel someone at our home, get someone out of jail, which required that we be sensitive and understand the demands of a pastor. As a child, it was disappointing not to have them there at school plays and other activities, but I learned to appreciate the times we did share. We came to realize that with the calling to pastor comes sacrifices. Nevertheless, Mom and Dad did the best they knew how to maintain and preserve our family in light of the requirements that come with a life of ministry.

I thank God that there were small, still moments away from ministry that afforded us the opportunity to grow in our Christian walk and to maintain family ties. There are several life lessons that I learned from my parents that were divinely orchestrated by God. First and foremost, I learned to have an unwavering faith and trust in God no matter what was going on in my life. I can't pinpoint the exact moment or time that I learned it, but it came from their example of trusting God to do the impossible when they were at the end of their ability. Through their example, I learned that we can do all things through Christ Jesus who strengthens us.

Another lesson I learned from my parents was to value family. I always took pride and joy in spending time with each of my family members, both individually and collectively. Even if it meant riding with Dad to the church for 45 minutes in total silence, I treasured those precious moments when I had him all to myself. He may not have said one word, but I knew in that silence that he loved me and I was his "Baby Girl."

One memory that remains with me today is from a Pastor's Anniversary celebration at the church. I was asked to sing a solo, and I dedicated the song "Order My Steps" to my Dad. God anointed me to sing the song in such a way that Dad and everybody else were blessed. However, what I found most endearing was the pride and joy he showed when we later reminisced about the afternoon service. Dad sat in his chair like a proud peacock and said, "Girl, you *know* you sang that song! It was like listening to a bird! I could've gone on to glory!" I remember leaping for joy in my heart, excited and glad that I had made my Dad proud. This was important to me, not only because I was his baby girl, but also because he had a love for singing and music, and to have him show such pride let me know I was doing something right! Truly, I wish he were here today to talk to about music and ministry.

Finally, the most important lesson I learned from Mom and Dad was that of love and commitment to family. Over the years, I watched my parents express their love for each other and show us how much they loved and cared for us and our extended family. The love they had for family was demonstrated by the family customs we established. For as long as I can remember, we always had dinner together every night at 6:00 PM, come rain or shine. Even when my mother worked a full-time job, she made sure there was a hot, home-cooked meal on the table for all to enjoy. While the dinner was the focal point, the main draw for dinner was the time for fellowship that we shared. We had the opportunity to laugh, bond and understand what it means to be a family, *our* family. Sometimes we kids would chip in and start dinner before Mom came home, but the result was a time for us to really connect with each other in the midst of life's chaos. In fact, we even reserved Friday nights as "Pizza Night". Mom and Dad had their pizza and we had our pizza. We made them together from scratch! This dinner ritual was extended to Sunday dinners as well, when Mom would pour over a hot stove for most of Saturday afternoon. In order to make sure her family was well fed, she made sure we transported the food down to our paternal grandmother Rebecca Harris's house or our maternal Grandma Tommie's house for Sunday afternoon. Unfortunately, after Dad died (and Grandma Rebecca shortly after him), all of the dinner rituals pretty much fell by the wayside. It grieved our hearts and spirits every time we gathered either at Mom's house or Grandma's — it was just too hard. Thankfully, over time God healed our wounds and allowed us to create new rituals that were somewhat different from what we knew but still let us know we were a family, no matter what.

I am thankful and grateful to God for placing me in such a loving, kind, and supportive family. We are living in a time where God and family have been lost in the shuffle of life.

I praise God that I come from parents who have shown me the value and benefits of putting Him and family first. I believe God and my parents have given me a blueprint for my own life, marriage, and family. While I have learned the most important and obvious lesson of putting God first in all things, I have learned the true meaning of family: love, life, and laughter. Whether in good times or bad, I know God and family are there for me when no one else is. Thank you Mom and Dad for all that you did, and do, for me and the rest of the children. I promise to instill in my future family and children the importance of being a God-loving and fearing family, and I commit myself to creating an atmosphere of love, life, and laughter during the good, the bad, and the ugly.

God bless you Mom and Dad!

– Tina M. Harris

The Mantle of Manhood

Dad was never a very talkative person, so when he *did* speak, you listened. I often heard him use quotes and witty sayings. Even though I didn't always understand what they meant, I could always tell when Dad was telling me to check my behavior. He just had a unique way of getting his point across. Even today, many of his words, quips, and clever remarks echo in my ears.

In his own unique way, Dad encouraged us to do well, to be the best we could be, to succeed. He impressed on us that in order to succeed one thing was necessary...education. He was a firm believer that education was something that couldn't be taken away from you, and that as an African-American in today's world, an education was essential to give you credibility. Dad assured me that I was just as intelligent and bright as others were, but he also instilled in me the desire to attain educational degrees as a reflection of my intellectual aptitude.

Since Dad began college late in life, I remember times when I was in school, and so was he. There were instances when we both had to "get our lesson", a term that denotes doing homework. From reading, studying, watching documentaries, and listening to National Public Radio on a regular basis, my father was a scholar in the true sense of the word. He passed his love of knowledge on to his children. The overarching theme, however, was not only to obtain a wealth of knowledge, but to disseminate it to those who weren't as fortunate to have it, to always seek more knowledge, and to get a deeper understanding. He allowed me to see that one can learn much, but will never learn it all.

I am the youngest of the children and was born when my father was 45 years old. Admittedly, I *might* have been spoiled a bit...a fact that I never have owned up to until this moment. Because I was the baby of the family and had suffered health complications as a young child, there were very few things that I asked for that I didn't receive. In spite of being catered to and treated extra special, my father's greatest concern was that I might grow up and not know how to live independently. He did not want me to become dependent on them, so he encouraged me to learn to stand on my own. However, it was not until after his death that I was able to do that.

Dad's death occurred when I was at a different place in life than my siblings. They were all adults, had left home, and were pursuing their own goals and aspirations. I, on the other hand, still lived at home, had only been 16 years old for a month, and actually was the one who found my father dead. Finding his lifeless body on the steps of our house is an event that is indelibly impressed in my mind; nevertheless, the lessons I learned immediately after his passing are invaluable life lessons that I may not have otherwise learned.

Contrary to popular belief, becoming a man is not something that is automatically acquired at a certain age, nor is it something that is attained through sexual conquests. I used to question God and ask Him why *I* had to be the one who found Dad, why I had to be the first one on the scene, and why I had to be haunted by images of my father's unresponsive body, slumped on our front stairs. I now understand that it was a rite of passage. There was a passing of the mantle from him to me. This mantle passing is analogous to the mantle that was passed from Elijah to Elisha in the Bible. I can honestly say that from the experience, I felt transformed from adolescence to manhood. Therefore, in his death, my father taught me how to be a man…a lesson that some fathers don't teach their sons even when enjoying a long lifespan together.

To say that my father was a phenomenal man is a complete understatement. I see his legacy living on in my older brothers, in my nephews, but more importantly, in myself. Though a small man in stature, he left some enormous shoes for me to fill; however, he left me with the love, training, wisdom and desire to do so. I honor my father, Rev. Joseph Harris, for modeling manhood to me. "Dad, I love you!"

— Ken Harris

Breaking the Curse

I am truly grateful to God that after all the tragic situations that occurred in my life and family, He has enabled me to move on and be an overcomer. I find great comfort in the fact that Joe and I raised four successful, healthy, prosperous, god-fearing children, who live blessed lives.

My life started out in a negative cycle of poverty, abuse, sexual transgressions and shame, but God gave me a vision of a better life. I dreamed of pulling myself out of the vicious circle of clandestine sexual encounters, and the humiliation and degradation that accompanied them, to become a woman of integrity and dignity. It has been a process, but I believed that I could do better, live better and have more than what I grew up with. I was determined to make changes in my family history. I wanted to do everything I could to break the stronghold of children born out of wedlock. The generational curse had gone on long enough and I knew God had a better way! I sought, through my children, to make a new legacy for our family, for my family tree to sprout new branches, to produce new growth and never to be plagued with the hidden truths of physical love without marriage.

The greatest confirmation of where God has brought victory to my dream is in the success of my children. They were raised in the church and taught the ways of the Lord at an early age, even when Joe and I were not as faithful as we should have been. They are intelligent, hard working and accomplished in their lives. I am very proud of all of them. Their success represents my victory and God's mercy: His having heard my cries during the many beatings I received, His hand on my life when I felt rejected at being left pregnant and alone, and His holding my hand when I experienced the pain of being ignored by the church that I loved. Through His love and grace, my family has moved from a tale of negativity to a place of victory and success. Undeniably, it is all because of the divine grace and mercy of God that we have no children born out of wedlock in my children's generation! In my heart of hearts, I believe that the generational curse has been broken! The shackles that once clenched our hearts, and sought to kill our joy, have been cast into the sea of forgetfulness, never to choke life out of the family again! God, we praise You!

— Pastor, Apostle Mamie Harris

MINISTRY TO THE WIDOWED

CHALLENGE TO PASTORS AND CHURCHES

My experience has given me insight into hurting widows and widowers. God has given me understanding of their needs. For most of us, it is often difficult to comprehend another person's problem unless we have walked in their shoes. My heart fully understands the path widows and widowers must walk. They don't fit perfectly into most singles ministries. Divorce recovery groups and married couples' fellowships are not appropriate; however, surviving spouses need to receive specific ministry. I challenge pastors and churches to establish ministry groups that help widows and widowers reestablish their lives. If a church determines that such a ministry is not suitable for them, as an alternative, they may want a team of people available to minister to widows, widowers and their families. Grief can be destructive when one has to endure it alone. Something as simple as a prayer, a hug or a phone call can give someone hope. The body of Christ is responsible for bringing healing, restoration and reconciliation to families, the backbone of the church.

Advance Preparation

When a family has prepared, the logistical and business aspects of losing a loved one will be easier. In preparation, I recommend the following:

➢ Keep a current will.

➢ Establish a durable power of attorney.

➢ Prepare a living will.

➢ Have a living trust (this will avoid probate and will replace a will).

➢ List material possessions and designate who you want to own them (you may want to write names on the back of pictures, furniture, etc.).

➢ Write a letter to your loved ones.

➢ Write your last wishes and make them known to a trustworthy friend (your children and spouse may not remember).

➢ Keep all essential papers together in a safe deposit box or a fire proof safe or file.

➢ Make a list of telephone numbers and addresses of your lawyer, minister, insurance companies, policy numbers, and investment groups.

➢ Identify a Certified Public Accountant for financial matters.

➢ Prepare a list of your closest friends with phone numbers.

Checklist for Surviving Spouses

A widow or widower is often faced with much emotional pain at the loss of their spouse. I have consolidated some important facts that I learned because of my own experience. This simple checklist will help one to prepare for life after their spouse passes.

➤ Make your immediate needs known to people who are equipped and willing to help you.

➤ Be honest and let people know that you are hurting.

➤ Be sensitive to the needs of your children.

➤ Respect your deceased spouse's siblings and your in-laws.

➤ Be prayerful before making any decisions, especially immediate decisions about your life, home, children and finances.

➤ Be careful with whom you share personal and confidential information. Understand that you are vulnerable at the time of your spouse's death, and information shared with the wrong person can harm or embarrass you later.

➤ Identify one person with whom you can trust to discuss personal matters.

➤ Avoid borrowing or lending money and be prayerful in giving.

➤ Allow ample time for yourself. Have a quiet place of solitude where you can rest and sort out your life.

➤ Allow sufficient time to grieve. It's okay to cry. Delayed grief may cause depression.

> ➢ Never discuss matters that will be embarrassing to the deceased.
> ➢ Trust God to meet your needs and not people. He will send people who will help you.
> ➢ Know who you are in Christ.
> ➢ Set realistic goals for your life.